Charles H Rector

The Story of Beautiful Porto Rico

A graphic description of the garden spot of the world by pen and camera

Charles H Rector

The Story of Beautiful Porto Rico
A graphic description of the garden spot of the world by pen and camera

ISBN/EAN: 9783337083335

Printed in Europe, USA, Canada, Australia, Japan

Cover: Foto ©ninafisch / pixelio.de

More available books at **www.hansebooks.com**

THE STORY
OF
BEAUTIFUL PORTO RICO

A GRAPHIC DESCRIPTION
OF
THE GARDEN SPOT OF THE WORLD
BY
PEN AND CAMERA

COMPRISING

The History, Geography, Soil, Climate, Inhabitants, Customs, Churches, Schools, Rivers, Lakes, Mountains, Mines, Products, Imports, Exports, Current Prices, Scenes of the Invasion, Railroads, Public Roads, Telegraph, Telephone, Money, Measures, Etc.

BY C. H. RECTOR

PROFUSELY ILLUSTRATED

With Nearly Sixty Half-Tone Reproductions from Fresh Photographs by the Celebrated Artist

WILBUR F. TURNER
AND
Two Maps Especially Designed for this Work

CHICAGO
LAIRD & LEE, PUBLISHERS
1898

Entered according to Act of Congress, in the year 1898,
BY WM. H. LEE,
in the office of the Librarian of Congress at Washington, D. C.

All Rights Reserved.

Dedicated

TO

OUR ARMY AND NAVY, PRESIDENT McKINLEY, HIS CABINET
AND THE PUBLIC WHO AIDED SO GENEROUSLY IN
ACHIEVING
THE TRIUMPHANT RESULTS OF THE
HISPANO-AMERICAN WAR.

INDEX

	PAGE
A Welcome	9
History of Porto Rico	13
Geography, Provinces and Population	21, 25
The Soil	38
The Climate	41
The Inhabitants	46
Schools and Education	50
Church and Religion	54
Products	57
Cattle, Fodder and Poultry	73
Insects, Game, Fish and Birds	78
Rivers, Lakes and Lagoons	82
Harbors	86
Mountains, Mines, Caves, etc.	90
Public Roads	97
Railroads and Street Cars	105
Telegraph and Telephones	113
Measures and Money	117
Miscellaneous Information	121
Peculiarities of Porto Rican Life	126
An Object Lesson	134
The Market of Ponce	137
The Capital	145
A Legend	149
An American Hero's Grave	154
The Red Cross	158
A Spanish Officer's Sword	161
A Typical Hacienda Owner	166
Spanish Sincerity	169
An Editor's View	174
Looking Backward	178
Looking Forward	183

INDEX TO ILLUSTRATIONS

	Page
General Miles in Ponce, Frontispiece.	
Map Showing Topography of Porto Rico,	8
Camp of the Sixth Illinois, at Ponce,	11
Company H, Sixteenth Penna. Vols., Before Abonito,	12
Street and Public Square, San German,	15
American War Vessels at Anchor in Guanica Bay,	16
San Antonio Bridges, San Juan,	19
Looking Across the Lagoon from San Juan,	20
The Only Protestant Church in Porto Rico,	23
Plaza and Cathedral at Arecibo,	24
Cathedral and Public Square in Mayaguez—Showing Statue of Columbus, and U. S. Cavalryman on Guard,	28
Bird's-Eye View of Ponce,	31
Plaza, or Public Square, Ponce,	35
Typical View Along the Highways,	39
A Garden in Porto Rico,	43
Group of Native Women and Children, Mayaguez,	47
Fire Engine House, Ponce,	48
View of San German—Natives in Foreground,	51
Cathedral, Ponce,	55
The Royal Palm,	59
Pack Train, Carrying Coffee to Market,	60
Sugar Cane Plantation,	63
Breaking Camp to Return Home,	67
Provisional Engineers (Officers of U. S. Volunteers),	71
A Grass Peddler,	75
After a Fishing Trip,	80
Street Scene in San German,	83

INDEX TO ILLUSTRATIONS.

	Page
Company "A," First Illinois,	84
A Train of Ox Carts, Carrying Army Supplies,	88
Battery "M," Seventh Artillery, Ready for Action,	92
The Famous Quintana Baths, Near Ponce,	95
A Mountain Trip by Pony Path,	99
Spanish Barracks in San Juan,	103
Railway Depot and Yard at Ponce,	107
Engine and Train, Narrow Gauge Road,	111
A Street in Ponce,	115
Hdqrs. of Gen's Miles and Wilson during Invasion,	119
Camp of Battery "C," Pennsylvania Volunteers,	123
The Porto Rican Milkman,	127
A Porto Rican Funeral Procession,	131
A View of Cemetery Vaults,	132
A Group of Spanish Officers and Soldiers,	135
Officers of the Sixth Illinois Volunteers,	136
Busy Scene in Market Place,	139
Market Hall, Ponce,	143
View of San Juan, Capital of Porto Rico,	144
Rear View of Morro Castle, San Juan,	147
Old Cathedral, Port Ponce—Camp of Battery "E," Pennsylvania Volunteers,	151
General View of Cemetery in Porto Rico,	155
Scene in a Spanish Hospital, San Juan,	159
Ambulances of the American Army,	160
Spanish Transports, San Juan Harbor,	163
A Rich Man's Plantation, and Driveway,	167
A Peon's Home Under Banana Trees,	168
Camp of Battery "M,"	171
American Boys Amusing Themselves After the Victory,	175
American War Ships in Guanica Bay,	179

WILBUR F. TURNER   CHARLES H. RECTOR

THE ABOVE CUTS faithfully picture the artist and author of "Beautiful Porto Rico." These gentlemen made a trip which practically covered the whole island, sailing around the greater part of the coast twice, and later traveling some three hundred miles inland by railroad, coach and native pony. They passed through fourteen towns while yet occupied by the Spanish army, having many thrilling experiences. They climbed to the mountain tops, and investigated the management of the great plantations where coffee is grown, and were unquestionably the first men to cover this entire territory and secure facts and figures on the ground, with no guesswork, and to secure life-like pictures of the natives, with their surroundings. The trip was full of risk, and many times they resorted to heroic measures to pass Spanish garrisons. At Abonito the Spanish Commander was induced to loan his private carriage to carry them out of the Spanish lines, which was a queer procedure in time of war. By making this successful trip these gentlemen are able to give to the world information never before published.

THE PUBLISHERS.

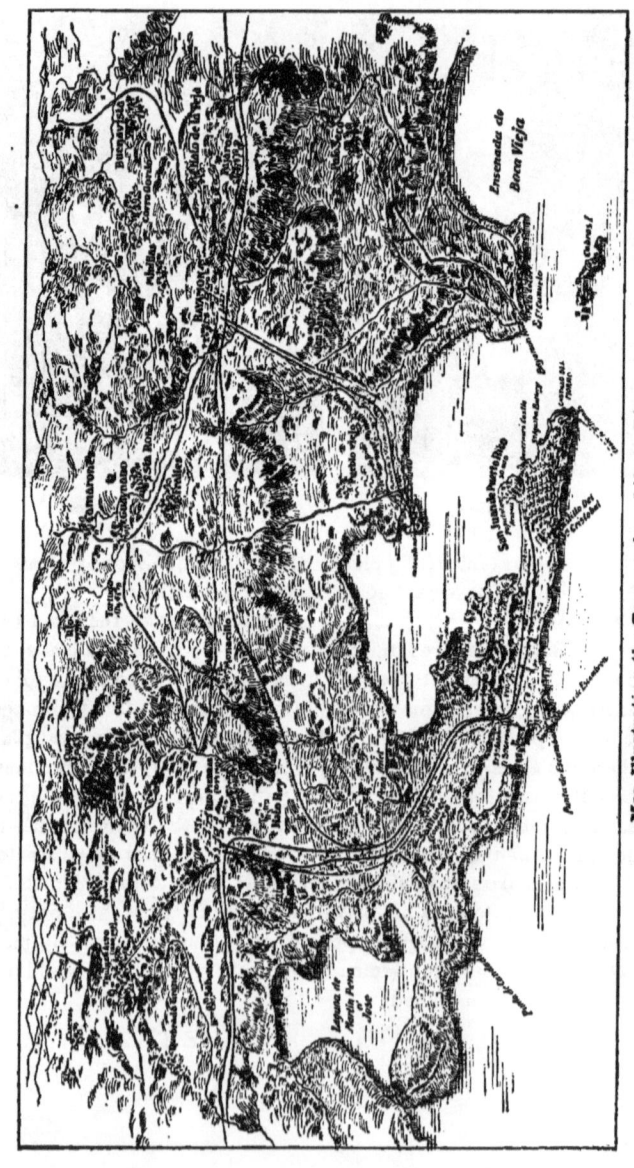
Map Illustrating the Topography of Porto Rico.
COPYRIGHT, 1898, BY WM. H. LEE.

A WELCOME.

When your brother marries a stranger in a distant land, you are happy to receive the likeness of the new sister, with a few lines descriptive of her features and complexion, and of her qualities.

Our family of States has just received an addition, Porto Rico. It is true we do not know yet what the status of the new member will be in our family, but she has come to stay, and it will be well to make her acquaintance.

I should like to introduce the reader, as I was introduced—sailing over the shining sea and beholding the island emerge suddenly out of a mist, a dazzling beauty. The sun suddenly dispersed the veil of vapors hiding her, and disclosed to our admiring eyes, beyond the flashing, dancing waters and against a deep blue sky, a gigantic and perfect garden. Were they trees or mountain tops? Rows behind rows of green wavy lines, rising from the very shore to a height of 4,000 feet and more. Who would not fall in love with such a picture? Could it be that there was suffering, injustice, oppression between those verdant hills? Surely, if there was a spot on earth where human beings might be just and kind and happy without great exertion, this must be the place. And if the notions and laws of the old regime are in the way of a peaceful and successful pursuit of happiness, we will wipe them out. Our new sister shall enjoy our liberty and will soon learn to love our ways.

Camps of the 6th Ills. Issuing Shoes to the Soldiers After a Hard March From Yauco to Ponce.

Company H, 16th Pennsylvania Vols. The Outpost of the American Army before Abonito, the Spanish Stronghold, September 4, 1898.

HISTORY OF PORTO RICO.

It was Columbus who discovered and named Porto Rico. On the 16th day of November 1493, during his second voyage, he sighted the island, disembarked and landed on the 19th day of the same month, and, struck by the beauty and fertility of the land, called it Puerto Rico, which signifies "Rich Port". Those of my readers who have seen with their own eyes what Columbus saw, will testify that Christopher evidently knew a good thing when he saw it, and was not at a loss for a suitable name. The natives called the island "Borinquen".

Sixteen years after the first discovery, in 1509, the Spanish established the first settlement on the island, Caparra, under Don Juan Ponce de Leon, and from that time on, a steady stream of Spaniards slowly but surely displaced the gentle Indian natives. The history of these Aborigines was the same pitiful tale, wherever the Spanish gained a foothold. In Porto Rico hardly a trace of the Indian blood is to be discovered among the population to-day. Caparra, the cradle of the "Puertoriquenos" was abandoned in 1552; its site is called Quebrada Margarita to-day. But as a lasting monument to the daring pioneer, the second city in importance of the island perpetuates his name, Ponce.

We give the dates of the settlement of all the principal places on the island later on, and confine ourselves here to an outline of the history of the whole island.

The capital, whose full name is San Juan Batista de Puerto Rico, was founded by Don Juan Ponce de Leon in 1511, the Casa Blanca being the first building erected.

In the same year, the town of San German, in the west of the island, was founded by Captain Miguel Toro. San German preserves, more than the capital, the features of the past. Its inhabitants are very proud of their quaint town and its history. Especially do they glory in relating an incident of the English

View of Street and Public Square in San German.

invasion of 1743, when the patriotic and valiant burghers of San German met the invaders half way between their city and Guanica Bay where the English had landed, (and where on July 25th, 1898, General Miles forced an entrance,) defeated them and drove them back into their ships.

For all that, they will be good American citizens. Sober and practical people, they have accepted their fate. When a gentleman in the author's company exhibited a tiny American flag, the Porto Ricans cheered lustily. If good judgment and tactful respect for their prejudices and habits are shown by our officials, they will be valuable citizens in the near future. In a little book, authorized by the Spanish Administration of Porto Rico, as a school book, the character of the inhabitants is stated to be "frank and expansive," and if this be a true estimation, they will blend well with the "Yankees" of these latter days, to be sure.

In all, the island was invaded nine times, owing to the "codicia" (covetousness) of the foreigners, as the little book referred to states. The French invaded the island in 1538. The English under Drake paid the island a visit and sacked the capital in 1595. Three years later, the Earl of Cumberland repeated the process with much zest. In 1625 Baldwin Heinrich, a Dutch Commander, lost his life in an attack on Castello del Mono. After that the English monopolized the business, swooping down on their prey in 1678, 1702, 1703, 1743 and, for the last time, in 1797.

In 1820, a movement was made toward a declaration of independence on the part of the Porto Ricans, but the Spanish stifled the rebellion and regained the upper hand in 1823.

In 1824, Commodore Porter of the United States, during his successful raids on the West Indian pirates, invaded the island, and seventy-five years later on, May 12th, 1898, Admiral Sampson appeared before San Juan and bombarded the ports during three hours. It is a coincidence worth noting, that on July 25th, the day when the rumor went abroad first that Spain was ready to yield to the inevitable, and when General Merritt reached Manila, the American forces under General Miles also landed at Guanica Bay, Porto Rico, hoisting the American flag over the town after an insignificant skirmish.

On August 11th, 1898, a protocol was signed at Washington, by the terms of which Spain ceded Porto Rico to the United States.

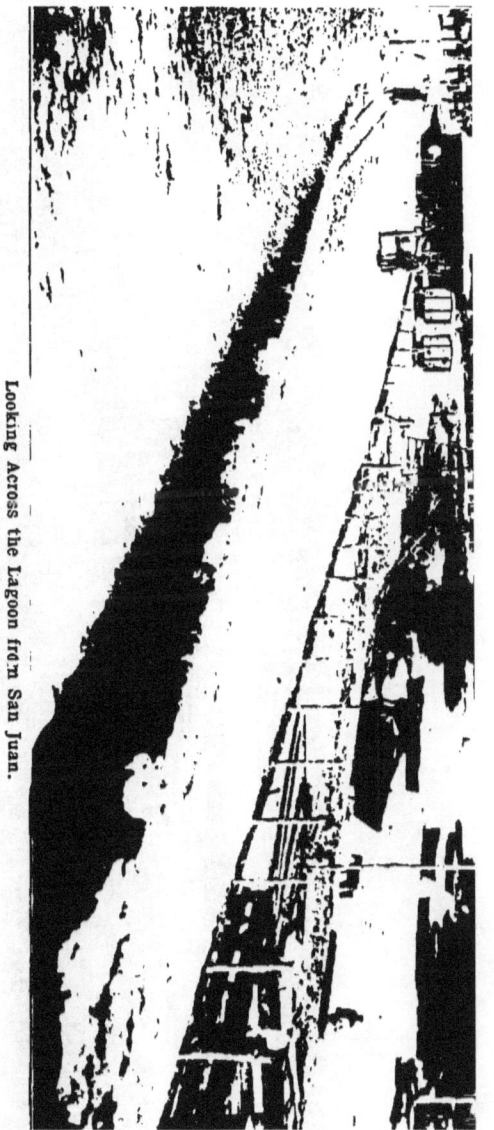
Looking Across the Lagoon from San Juan.

San Antonio Bridges, San Juan.

GEOGRAPHY.

On October 18th, 1898, General Brooke took formal possession of the island. The simple ceremonies of raising the flag over San Juan, the capital, included music by the military bands and the firing of guns.

GEOGRAPHY.

Porto Rico is situated between longitude 9 degrees 44 minutes and 11 degrees 25 minutes east from Washington and between latitude 17 degrees 54 minutes and 18 degrees 30 minutes 40 seconds north. It is bounded on the north by the Atlantic ocean, on the east and south by the Sea of the Antilles, and on the west by Mona Channel. The island is ninety-five miles long and thirty-five miles broad, with an estimated area of 3,668 square miles. According to the census of 1887, the population was 813,937, of which more than 300,000 were negroes. There are 137 miles of railway, about 150 miles of wagon road, 470 miles of telegraph lines and telephone systems.

San Juan, the capital, on the northern coast, is situated upon a small island connected with the main land by a substantial arched stone bridge, named San

Antonio, and also two iron railroad bridges. At the extremity of the island are the high cliffs which support El Morro Castle (Morro means round, and signifies, therefore, the old fashioned fort, as we see it on Governor's island, New York harbor, and in Castle Garden, New York.)

Ponce, a great mercantile center and the second city of importance, is about two miles from the south coast. It was the residence of a military commander and the seat of an official chamber of commerce. The only Protestant church in the Spanish West Indies is here. The little book already spoken of teaches that Porto Rico enjoys "tolerancia de cultos" (religious tolerance), but this church was found tightly closed by our soldiers. Playa is the city's seaport, and is considered the healthiest spot on the island, and second port in importance.

Mayaguez, the third city, is situated in the west part. It exports sugar, coffee, oranges, pineapples and cocoanuts. The annual export of coffee, ranging in price with Java, is 170,000 hundredweights. Of the 180,000 bags of flour that the island buys annually from the United States, 50,000 are imported into Mayaguez.

The Only Protestant Church in Porto Rico.

Plaza and Cathedral at Arecibo.

PROVINCES AND POPULATION. 25

Other principal cities, all ports, are Aquadilla on the north-west, Arecibo on the north coast, Fajardo and Nagabo on the east side, and Arroyo on the south-east.

Detailed information about rivers, mountains, railroads, etc., will be found under special headings. See index.

PROVINCES AND POPULATION.

Each town had jurisdiction over the immediate neighborhood in which it was located, and below is given the population of the jurisdiction, together with the year in which the town was founded and the total number of plantations of various kinds in the province, according to the directory of the island and other official records.

BAYAMON PROVINCE.

Name.	Year Founded.	Population.
Bayamon	1772	15,316
Corozal	1795	9,652
Dorado	1842	3,985
Loiza	1719	9,600
Naranjito	1824	6,631
Rio Piedras	1774	11,042

PROVINCES AND POPULATION.

Name.	Year Founded.	Population.
Rio Grande	1840	6,237
Carolina	1857	11,042
Toa-Alta	1751	6,808
Toa-Baja	1745	3,285
Trujillo Alto	1801	4,015
Vega-Alto	1775	5,498
Vega-Baja	1776	10,648
Total population		103,789

Cane plantations, 88; coffee, 275; fruits, 2,446.

ARECIBO PROVINCE.

Name	Year Founded	Population
Arecibo	1778	29,722
Camuy	1807	9,181
Ciales	1820	13,036
Hatillo	1823	9,671
Barceloneta	1882	6,246
Manati	1838	8,191
Morovis	1818	11,567
Quebradillas	1823	5,929
Utuado	1789	31,292
Total population		124,835

Cane plantations, 38; coffee, 396; tobacco, 66; fruits, 2,849.

Cathedral and Public Square in Mayaguez. Statue of Columbus in Center of Square, with American Cavalryman on Guard.

PROVINCES AND POPULATION.

AGUADILLA PROVINCE.

Name.	Year Founded.	Population.
Aguadilla	1775	13,306
Aguada	1511	9,557
Isabela	1819	12,554
Lares	1829	17,163
Moca	1774	11,092
San Sebastian	1752	14,042
Rincon	1770	5,837
Total population		83,551

Cane plantations, 40; coffee, 300; fruits, 2,394.

MAYAGUEZ PROVINCE.

Name	Year Founded	Population
Mayaguez	1760	28,246
Anasco	1703	12,437
Cabo Rojo	1771	16,844
Sabana Grande	1814	9,611
San German	1511	19,933
Las Marias	1871	9,792
Hormigueros	1876	3,199
Maricao	1876	7,728
Lajas	1883	9,192
Total population		116,982

Cane plantations, 90; coffee, 778; fruits, 2,535.

PONCE PROVINCE.

Name.	Year Founded.	Population.
Ponce	1752	42,705
Adjuntas	1815	16,321
Aibonito	1825	6,397
Barranquitas	1803	5,828
Barros	1825	11,697
Coamo	1646	10,537
Guayanilla	1833	7,805
Juana Diaz	1798	21,032
Penuelas	1793	10,023
Santa Isabel	1841	3,384
Yauco	1756	24,411

Total population.................... 160,140

Cane plantations, 49; coffee, 7,453; tobacco, 570; fruits, 9,260

Bird's-eye View of Ponce.

GUAYAMA PROVINCE.

Name.	Year Founded.	Population.
Guayama	1730	13,648
Arroyo	1855	6,040
Aguas-Buenas	1838	6,844
Caguas	1775	15,031
Cayey	1774	12,452
Cidra	1809	6,365
Gurabo	1815	7,202
Juncos	1797	7,414
Hato-Grande	1811	12,738
Salinas	1851	4,314
Sabana del Palmar	1826	6,739
Total population		98,787

Cane plantations, 38; coffee, 2,034; tobacco, 40; fruits, 3,563.

PROVINCES AND POPULATION.

HUMACAO PROVINCE.

Name.	Year Founded.	Population.
Humacao	1793	14,936
Ceiba	1838	4,314
Fajardo	1774	8,794
Luquillo	1797	6,579
Maunabo	1799	5,823
Naguabo	1794	9,914
Patillas	1811	10,553
Piedras	1801	8,028
Yabucoa	1793	13,103
Isle de Vieques	1843	6,019

Total population.................... 88,063

Cane plantations, 60; coffee, 317; fruits, 1,892.

COMBINED POPULATION OF PROVINCES.

San Juan, by last census	32,800
Bayamon, by old census report	103,789
Arecibo, by old census report	124,835
Aguadilla, by old census report	83,551
Mayaguez, by old census report	116,982
Ponce, by old census report	160,140
Guayama, by old census report	98,787
Humacao, by old census report	88,063

Total population.................... 818,947

Plaza or Public Square, Ponce.

The figures given above of the population will vary somewhat when the new census of the island is published. In a few of the towns I looked up the official figures, which were completed but not published, and found an increase in every instance.

In regard to the number of plantations given, it should be noted that those referred to as fruit plantations are almost all small patches. Some of the coffee and cane plantations are large, or fair in size, and much of the land is held by large owners and leased or rented on conditions long established in the island.

In many instances the cane land has not been worked of late years. Much of it is idle or used for grazing. This industry will certainly be much more extensively carried on now. In fact, a great increase may be made in all the products of the island, and this result may be confidently expected. It takes time to bring coffee, cocoanuts and such to a bearing state, but there is still room for planting, and with the whole United States as a market, the prospects of this garden, called Porto Rico, must be admitted to be bright indeed.

THE SOIL.

The island undoubtedly is of volcanic origin. The soil generally is clay, red in color, closely resembling the waste found around a brickyard where red brick is made. In the bottoms of the numberless valleys the decaying vegetable matter has accumulated and formed an alluvial stratum of darker hue. The fertility of the soil is marvellous. The use of fertilizers is unknown, because entirely unnecessary. The visitor is struck, as Columbus was, with the luxurious vegetation. The lowlands, especially in the south, are covered with sugar-cane fields, lined with cocoanut palms, the hill-sides are one mass of orange, lemon and lime orchards, interspersed with fields of pineapples and palm forests. The rocky tops of the hills and mountains are crowned by the coffee plantations. Banana trees grow everywhere. The rich deep green of the scenery is relieved and set off by a superabundance of the most gorgeous flowers and blossoms. Some of the flowers grow in clusters fully a yard long, hanging down from large beautiful trees by the thousand, and are in blossom the year around.

Spring reigns perpetually, and there are three or four harvest seasons during the year.

Typical View Along the Highways.

No cereals, such as wheat, rye or oats, are raised; these thrive better under a Minnesota sky. The potatoes, grown in small quantities, are of an inferior quality.

THE CLIMATE.

The temperature, as must be expected in the torrid zone, is always high, but the island, being so small, is swept in its whole extent by an almost constant sea-breeze from the north-east. In consequence, the mercury rarely rises above 86 degrees Fahrenheit (30 degrees Cent.), nor does it sink below 59 degrees Fahrenheit (15 degrees Cent.). The highest point ever reached in the last five years was 92 degrees.

The hot season sets in about July 1st, and lasts till the latter part of September. The rainy season commences in the latter part of August, and ends in December. During the heated term the morning hours are the hottest part of the day. By 10 o'clock a strong sea-breeze brings relief, and, together with the plentiful shade everywhere, renders life very comfortable.

The rainy season is not as terrible as many people imagine. It does not rain incessantly, but there are frequent heavy showers, after which the sky clears again in surprising rapidity. As the island is one mass of hills, and even the southern plane is inclined seaward, the torrents of rain disappear as suddenly as they come. In an incredibly short time all is dry again, and everything greener and fresher for the shower-bath. Nor do the inhabitants seem to mind a drenching. There is no chill, and the light clothing dries quickly on the body, if a change is too troublesome. Violent windstorms or tornadoes are unknown; none is recorded after the year 1828.

Porto Rico is one of the most healthful spots on the globe. With proper judgment in eating of the tropical fruits, and if care is taken not to sleep in a draught, no fear need be entertained of fevers and other diseases peculiar to this latitude. To sleep in a draught, however, be it ever so slight, seems to be fatal. Colds and catarrh, consumption and bronchitis are common ailments among the natives.

The sanitary arrangements on the island are not in keeping with American ideas, but the abundance of running water and the natural slope of the ground toward the sea, in all directions, has been a natural substitute for artificial sewerage and draining, so that the conditions are not so bad, in spite of the customs

Typical View of a Garden in Porto Rico.

THE CLIMATE.

and habits of an indolent population. The capital, San Juan, is just building an aqueduct, very much needed. The city stands on a small island, and the houses are built closely together, having two stories each, which is unusual in Porto Rico. At present the people of the capital depend for their water supply entirely upon rain-water, caught upon the flat roofs and conducted to the cistern, which occupies the greater part of the inner court-yard, (the essential part of every Spanish house the world over, but here exceedingly small on account of the narrow confines of the island). Another large part of the court (patio) is occupied by the vault (cesspool), and, of course, its close proximity to the cistern is a source of frequent epidemics.

American enterprise is sure to introduce at once modern ideas as to sewerage, surface draining and aqueducts, stamping out all fevers; and a sure cure for the bronchial and lung troubles of the natives may be found in a little healthful physical exercise, to which your Porto Rican at present is a perfect stranger. The lack of muscular exertion, together with the effects of the everlasting cigar or cigarette, and the enormous amount of strong coffee consumed daily, have left the

Porto Rican a poor specimen of manhood. Outdoor exercise, embracing athletics, football, etc., will be among the greatest blessings that we can bring to them.

THE INHABITANTS.

In complexion the inhabitants of the island vary from a very deep black to a light brown. The colored people represent the darker shades and the Spaniards the lighter, but a real coal-black African is just as rarely to be found as a really white member of the white race.

In character, language, actions and gestures, the Spanish and the native Porto Rican are not distinguishable to an American eye. The men are spare in build, with a fair average in height. Owing to their indolent life, they are not muscular, but straight in carriage, and lively in manners, and the author found them frank and generous. Their little island is too small ever to be a kingdom or republic by itself, and so they have felt the heartburns of the Cuban patriot but little, nor have they ever been jealous or envious of other nations. Friendly with all the world, satisfied with their country, without a possible national ambition, and by

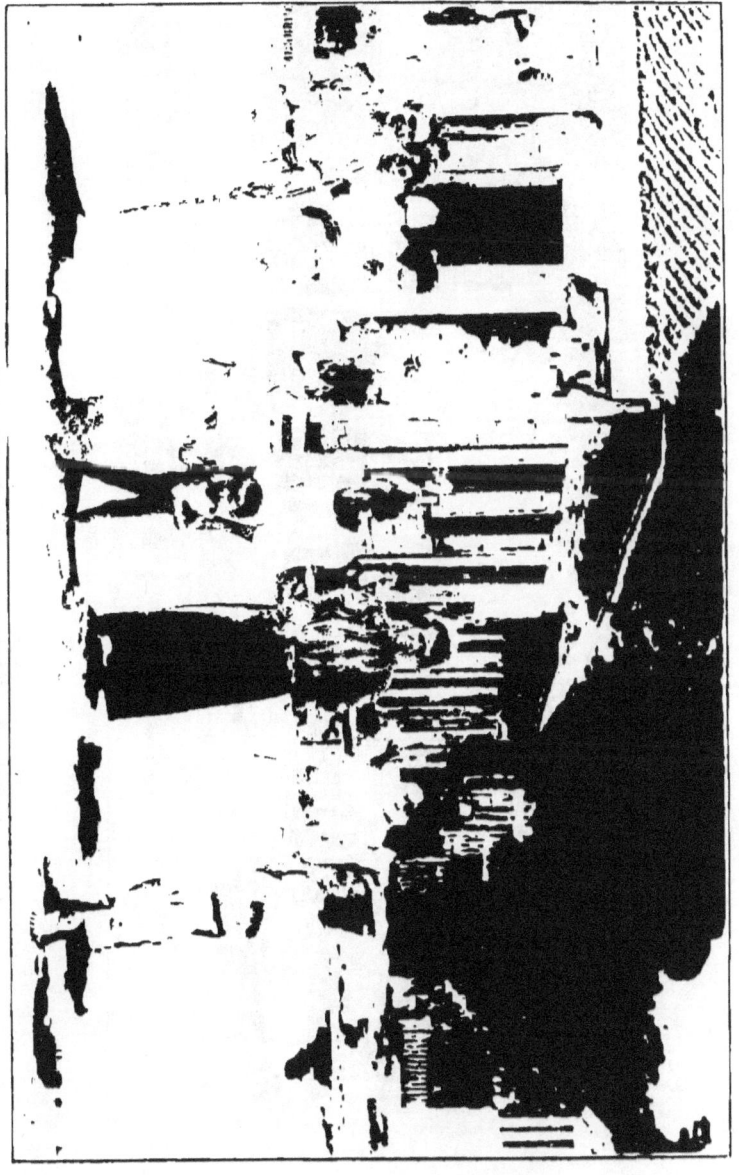
Group of Native Women and Children, Mayaguez.

"Fire Engine House, Ponce.

the very nature of their country compelled and enabled to trade with anybody and everybody, they are cosmopolitan in their hearts and were ready to become Americans, as they knew that the change would only tend to enhance their liberties without threatening a single one of their interests. This seems to be the natural explanation of the cordial reception with which our American boys and our flag met down there at their first appearance, so surprising to ourselves and all the world, and especially to the people of Spain, who could not understand it, since the Porto Ricans had not rebelled against the mother country but once, and that so long ago that hardly one in a thousand had ever heard of it.

The author found the men he met socially pleasant, generous and eager to please, gentlemanly in every respect. They lack some of the qualities of the stalwart American type, but this is due to their civic conditions. Without a voice in the government of state, district or city, without a voice in matters pertaining to church or school, taxes or tariff, they lack all political training and their horizon is limited by that much. The laborers and lower classes are no doubt lazier than their Northern brethren, but if we take into account the climate and the impossibility under Spanish rule to ever rise by the work of their hands, we may entertain the hope that under the American flag widened chances will spur them into greater and remunerative activity.

The fair sex in Porto Rico is of the same dark complexion as the men. They are as a rule plump and good-looking. Beyond this I cannot say, having seen but little of them during my hurried travels. Of the children I saw more, in fact all there could be seen in most cases. Up to their sixth or seventh year they wear no clothes at all, but run around "clad in innocence." Their plays are quieter than those of our boys and children, but the author frequently noticed their jolly good-naturedness.

SCHOOLS AND EDUCATION.

According to statistics there are 445 primary schools in Porto Rico, 299 for boys and 146 for girls, attended by 31,541 pupils of both sexes. It is stated that attendance is compulsory, instruction free to the poor, and they are furnished books, paper, etc., free of charge.

In view of this official statement, it was surprising to

Street View in San German, with Natives in the Foreground, and the Old Dominican Monastery, Nearly 400 Years Old, in the Background.

SCHOOLS AND EDUCATION.

find that so few people could either read or write, according to an estimate by a Porto Rican, in a position to be well informed, only about 7 per cent. of the population. Even if we do not assume that compulsory education exists on paper only, like religious tolerance, it will be possible to reconcile the two facts, by considering that the schools are entirely under the guidance of the Catholic Church, and that the greater part of the school hours is devoted to the instruction and drill of the children in the ceremonial and devotional exercises of the Catholic ritual, and to the legends of saints and martyrs, for all of which neither reading or writing is required.

The school buildings which we saw, were of the poorest possible description, some of them hardly deserving to be called anything better than a shed. Scores of fine cathedrals and the substantial guard-houses for the soldiers on the royal highways formed a significant contrast to these apologies for school houses.

The introduction of the American public school system will work a radical change in this most important matter. It will take some time to find and prepare the proper teachers, however, because they must speak

Spanish and pronounce it well, or the children will not understand them; but we should lose no time in planning and starting the great work.

Institutions for secondary education are scarce on the island.

CHURCH AND RELIGION.

The Roman Catholic Church religion is the only one existing in Porto Rico. It is the official or state religion and the churches and the clergy are supported by the state from general taxes. The island has a bishop who is subordinate to the archbishop of Santiago de Cuba.

We, in the United States, have no conception of the manner in which the whole public and private life in countries exclusively catholic, is pervaded by the intimate relations to the clergy.

We took pains to get the opinion of the Porto Ricans as to the effect of the imminent arrival of American protestant missionaries, and were surprised to find much indifference.

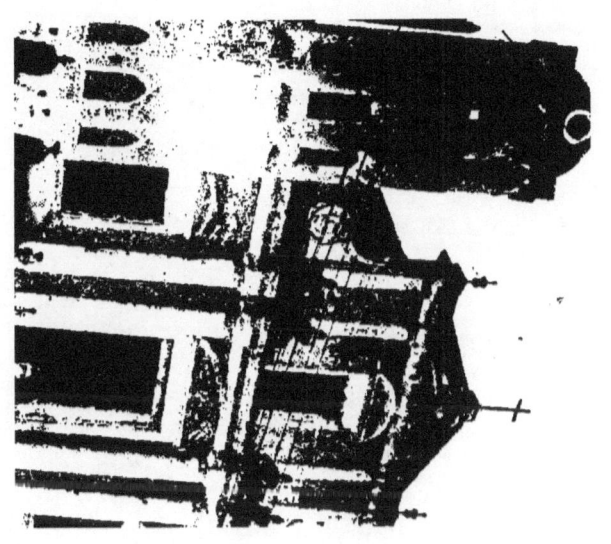

PRODUCTS.

The principal products of Porto Rico are sugar, coffee, tobacco, and cocoanuts, but the variety of fruits and vegetables outside of these named are almost innumerable, oranges, lemons, limes, pineapples, bananas, alligator pears, mangoes, papas, mamas and guavas, and of vegetables, beans, rice, corn, sweet potatoes, and almost every vegetable that grows in our land. All are plentiful. Wheat, rye, oats and barley must be imported; the potatoes raised are of a poor quality.

The time it takes various fruits and vegetation to bear or mature differs greatly. The coffee tree takes four years to produce, and then the yield is small, and not till the tree is seven years old is it counted at its best. Before planting coffee a plentiful shade must be provided. For the first two years a temporary shade is furnished by banana trees, and after that larger trees are planted and trained to give a permanent shade.

Passing through a coffee plantation is like going through a jungle. The large shade trees on an old plantation give it the appearance of a forest, and then the growth of coffee trees beneath their greater friends, spread and bend, till the narrow space of nine or ten feet between is covered and the branches intertwine and weave together, forming one thick mass of shrubbery. Beneath all this you will find another growth of vegetation in grass, flowers, vines, etc., and with this bottom mat, the dense shade and the almost daily rains, the coffee grove is always wet, and you cannot pass through without being draggled. A new plantation gives some returns after the fourth year. After the seventh year a good plantation is a gold mine for twenty-five years to come.

The trees are planted about three Spanish yards or varas apart, (a vara is about 33 inches), and an acre is about 75 varas square, which will make about 625 coffee trees to an acre. I could get no reliable information as to what the yield was per acre, but the profit is known to be very large. The trees grow about eight feet high and send out new shoots from the ground in different directions, and each and every stem is loaded with the highly-prized berries, each berry containing two of what we term grains of coffee. The stem is the size of a lead pencil, or less, and practically lined from end to end with berries. The berries will grow to the length of half an inch and a little less in diameter, being somewhat oblong, holding a rich,

The Royal Palm.

Pack Train Carrying Coffee to Market from the Mountain Plantations.

dark green color till ripening time, about the 1st of October, when they turn a bright rich red color. Their brittle skin contains a kind of jelly around the two grains of coffee. The skin is broken by a machine and the coffee is washed and cleansed of all adherent matter, and then dried on racks or cement beds in a few hours and is ready for the market. Porto Rican coffee is as good as any in the world and commands a price equal to that of Java.

There are excellent coffee plantations in the island that are miles up the mountains, being accessible only by little native pack ponies over mountain paths. The life of a coffee planter is not so bad when you think of the value of the crop, as a little pony will carry out at one time from a hundred to one hundred and fifty pounds of coffee, which means to the owner of the hacienda from 20 to 30 dollars. This may look to some as a slow life, but it very closely resembles a gold mine as the years go on. The exportation of coffee out of Porto Rico by the last published report for one year was $8,789,788 worth. Sugar cane is the next crop in value in Porto Rico. This crop will bear in nine months after planting, and will produce well for about seven years thereafter without replanting. It is a valuable crop. The fields seem to be covered so thick that there could not be found room for any more stalks. The discouraging conditions in the island the last few years have told more on the sugar industry than on anything else, and today there may be seen many fine cane plantations lying idle, and the buildings falling to decay, which show plainly by their architecture and extent that they have seen prosperous times. Acres and acres of sugar land are today given up to grazing of immense herds of native cattle, as the cultivating in years past was found to be unprofitable. There seems to be nothing different in the appearance of the cane when growing, or the management of an estate, from what we see in our own cane fields of Louisiana. This business will beyond any doubt take on new life now, and perhaps our occupation of this territory will tell more on the sugar trade than on any other business of the island. Sugar haciendas are quite plentiful along the coast and river valleys, and when encouraged, and properly cultivated, will, like the coffee, be a gold mine. The land today is held at from $100 to $200 per acre—American money—but the prices may vary from this when some basis for business is established there. The last report

Sugar Cane Plantation. The Planter's House, and the Sugar Mill in the Background.

published of the value of one year's sugar product exported, was $3,747,891. This amount will probably be doubled, when the industry takes new life.

Tobacco is a paying crop and is cultivated about the same as in the states. It is not grown to such an extent as sugar and coffee, only $646,556 worth being exported in one year, according to last published report. It is a strong tobacco when made into cigars, and it may be possible to improve it by proper curing. On the high lands in the vicinity of Coamo and Abonito are the best tobacco plantations.

Cocoanuts are a staple in the markets. They are used by the thousand, by the people of the island, and are exported in great quantities. A person owning one hundred acres of cocoanut trees, need not do any work the balance of his natural life. A tree will grow in about ten square feet, and this would give about 500 trees to the acre, and each tree is valued at from one dollar to one dollar and seventy-five cents each year. This is for the nuts alone, without considering the fiber that can be taken from the tree. It takes a tree from five to seven years to mature and bear, and it is said that a cocoanut tree was never known to die of its own accord. They live and yield continuously for almost countless years, are pretty to look at and rich in production.

Orange trees will bear in about four years. The fruit is fine and will perhaps prove worthy of cultivation.

Lemon trees will bear in about four years. Limes are grown quite extensively and are much more in use in Porto Rico than lemons.

The banana in Porto Rico comes nearer being at home everywhere, than any other fruit or vegetable. From the lowest lowlands to the highest hilltops the banana tree may be found, and apparently happy with its load of rich fruit. It is the best friend of the people who occupy this land. Its fruit is plentiful and holds about the same place there that our potatoes hold here. The people would find life hard without them. They have many varieties, which are used in different ways. The one that is eaten raw as we eat bananas, grows in small clusters and only about five inches long. It is fine of meat and rich in flavor. From this variety they run up to great size and length; and the larger ones are much coarser and are used for cooking and also drying and rubbing into flour. The tree will grow to its height from nine to fifteen feet, and bear in

United States Soldiers Breaking Camp to Start Home, September 7, 1898.

about nine months. It is rich and beautiful to look at and gives good shade.

Pineapples grow in abundance. They bear fruit in about nine months, grow very large and are of the best flavor and quality. Will be a paying staple and require little labor, as the same plant produces fruit many times in succession. The pineapple culture is likely to be one of the leading industries of the island.

Grapes are grown but little. The grape vine seems to thrive better in the temperate zone where the plant gathers strength during the winter season.

The guava is a small fruit, growing on a tree like a peach or apple tree, about one and a half inches in diameter. Nearly round in shape with seeds like a tomato or fig. This fruit is used extensively to make a jelly or paste. Occasionally it is found in our markets. Because of the plentifulness of the fruit and the rich pleasant paste that can be made from it, a guava-jelly industry is sure to spring up and this delicacy will soon find a place by the side of our other sweetmeats.

Alligator pears are plentiful and much used by the natives. They grow on large trees and are offered for sale in abundance in the markets and by peddlers.

They are three times the size of our large California pears, dark green in color and coated with a hard shell-like skin. The taste is not much like that of our pear and in first trying to eat the fruit one may pronounce it a poor pear, but a good kind of pumpkin. Cooking or preserving may bring out its hidden virtues. Beside the fruits named there are many others, such as the mango, which the natives use extensively, but which proved to be very unhealthy to our soldiers while doing service in Porto Rico. The fruit is large, reddish yellow in color, and grows on large trees in abundance. Then there is the cactus fruit, the mama, the canape and innumerable others.

It is a land of fruits of all kinds and in the greatest abundance. In addition to the fruits, vegetables of all kinds are plentiful. Sweet potatoes and beans are excellent. The Porto Rican rice is of a variety that does not require so much water as the Louisiana rice. Corn is good and three crops may be grown in one year. Almost all the vegetables familiar to us are found on the north side of the island and well up to the high lands.

For a person with a love for a grand garden with

Officers of Provisional Engineers in Porto Rico, Composed of Company A, First Illinois, and Washington, D. C. Company, in their Kitchen at the Base of a Large Tree while in Camp Near Ponce.

fruits, flowers and vegetables, by the side of running water, Porto Rico is the place, especially the northern portion.

CATTLE, FODDER AND POULTRY.

The stock and poultry of Porto Rico are very inferior. You will find poor horses or, rather, no horses, but little ponies weighing 600 or 700 pounds. The cattle are fair in size, up to the average of ours, but not the best for milk or meat. The oxen of the island are perhaps superior to our own, as they are so muscular and strong in the neck, having been bred for the purpose of drawing heavy loads. The yoke is tied to the horns by rawhide thongs, and the loads on the two-wheeled cart are pushed up-hill and controlled going down-hill by their great necks.

Draught oxen are worth from 125 to 200 pesos a yoke, according to the quality of the stock, the excellence of the match and the care with which they have been broken, of course. Good beef is scarce and brings in good times $3\frac{1}{4}$ or $3\frac{1}{2}$ pesos for the arroba (25 pounds).

The principal varieties of pasture grass grown in

Porto Rico are guinea grass, para and gramma. The first does not require a rich soil and grows on the hills. Cut and chopped it makes an excellent green fodder. Gramma is about the same, while para requires the rich, alluvial soil of the bottom land. It fattens the cattle, but does not give them much solid flesh.

Cattle raisers have to contend with two pests, the guava and a peculiar plant called "mori vivi." The guava is eaten by the cattle with avidity. The undigested seeds are scattered everywhere, take root, and, growing and multiplying rapidly, are more destructive to a pasture than the thistle of the north. The "mori vivi" is a sensitive plant which it is hard to fight. The center of the little weed is a tempting morsel for cattle, but it is surrounded by a circular row of very sharp and stiff needles, which usually lie flat on the ground, but rise like the bristles of a porcupine as soon as a cow or steer attempts to nibble at it. The cattle soon learn not to poke their noses into these prickles and the weed, unmolested, soon overruns the whole pasture, so that it has to be abandoned for a whole season at times, until these pests can be exterminated.

Cured hay is unknown on the island, as green fodder

A Grass Peddler.

CATTLE, FODDER AND POULTRY.

is abundant all the year around. In the cities the grass peddler makes his daily rounds, like a milkman.

The other animals found on the island, like the goat, sheep, hog, dog, etc., seem to be dwarfed and need new blood to bring them up to a useful state and to the size that is common with us. The hog can beat the long-nosed Mississippi rooter in leanness and length of head.

The poultry, like the animals, are of inferior grade. The chicken, which is so useful to man, is very small in size. It looks like a species of game, not so large, but even leaner, if possible. The little cock of the chicken family is as proud as a Spaniard, and being trained for the pit, would put up a good fight, as some of our army officers, who turned to this sport in their leisure hours, will testify.

Turkeys are small. They do not seem to take on any meat and are almost unfit for use, nor can you ever call a Porto Rican turkey pretty, as it is generally as innocent of plumage as the children are of clothes.

This state of things was certainly brought about by the island being cut off from the balance of the world, and no new blood being taken into the community. For four centuries they have been inbred and inbred, till they are so diminutive in size that they are almost worthless. It is a grand opportunity for our stock breeders to try experiments and see what the country needs and what will thrive there, and fill this one void in Porto Rico as we found it.

INSECTS, GAME, FISH AND BIRDS.

There are no snakes in the island of any consequence; only very small and perfectly harmless specimens are to be found.

Centipedes are quite plentiful, but are not much dreaded by the people. The peons go barefoot and seem to have no fear of them. They are found principally about old buildings. Their sting is not counted fatal.

The tarantula is also to be found there, but I never came in contact with one, and know of no case of our soldiers being disturbed by them in all their camping in low land and on mountain side, and I do not think they will seriously interfere with the enjoyment of life.

The lizard is common and may be seen in all its glory along the road, and of all colors; perfectly harmless to any one that is not too nervous. If you are

After a Fishing Trip.

nervous, you may find your peace broken by feeling one of them glide gently over your neck when in bed. There being no game on the island, it is no place for the hunter. I was told, though, that this class might find entertainment enough by simply crossing Mona channel to Mona island, about thirty miles distant, where wild hogs and goats and other game are plentiful.

Fish are abundant around the coast and many are caught, but there is no great business done in this line, as the climate is too warm to handle fish without ice, which is scarce.

While lying at anchor in Ponce and Mayaguez, we saw many large fish in the water around the vessel, and some officers aboard amused themselves shooting at sharks. Whether there are any fish in the rivers I cannot say from my own knowledge, but I should judge that trout and similar fish would enjoy those mountain brooks and rushing rivers.

Birds are not very plentiful; those seen are very pretty: the parrot, the canary, the nightingale, the thrush, and many others.

RIVERS, LAKES AND LAGOONS.

I know of no other land on the globe so plentifully blest with pretty little fresh-water rivers as is this island. In her small area of less than 4,000 square miles, and where the whole island may be girdled by a trip of 275 miles, we find over sixty rivers pouring into the seas. None of these are large in the sense in which we of the land of the Mississippi, Ohio and Hudson speak of large rivers, but they gather quite a volume of water in their short course.

They form high up in the mountains from fresh-water springs, and, joining forces with many little streamlets and increased by the frequent rains, they become of volume enough to float a good-sized boat by the time they reach the coast.

There are three rivers of considerable importance. The Loiza, rising in Cerro-Gordo, near Cayey, passing through the districts of San Lorenzo, Caguas, Gurabo and the two Trujillos, emptying into the Atlantic ocean in the north of Loiza.

The Plata, rising in the Cayey district, on the Pelado range, passing through the districts of Cayey, Aibonito, Cidra, Sabana del Palmar, Naranjito, the two

Street Scene in San German. River, Valley and Mountains in the Background.

Company A, of 1st Ills., Grouped on Temporary Bridge Built by Them Near Ponce.

RIVERS, LAKES AND LAGOONS.

Toas, and El Dorado emptying into Boca-Habana, in the north of Lower Toa.

The Anasco, rising in San German, on the northern side of the Cain range, emptying in the west of the island.

Of some importance are, also, the Bayamon, Manati and Arecibo in the north; the Culebrinas and Guanajibo in the west, and the Jacaguas and Patillas in the south.

This wonderful supply of water for so small a territory is certainly worthy of comment. It is to this wealth of water and its perfect distribution throughout that the island owes its beauty and fertility. There is no place where the dry season or dry weather ever affects the crops, except in the south-east corner. It is here, perhaps, that the enterprising American may find a splendid field for the exercise of his genius and energy.

There need not be a crop failure on account of a drought if the water is properly husbanded, and the swift currents can easily be harnessed and made to turn the wheels of industry, or produce an electric current that will propel the trolley car even to the mountain peaks, or give light to the homes that are now lighted by the crude tallow dips that we delegated to the past so many generations ago.

There is a lagoon running east from Arecibo about one mile inland, about four miles long, which will float a good-sized vessel. Several small inland lakes may be found along the coast, principally on the north side.

HARBORS.

Guanica Bay is on the south side of the island and well to the west. It is beyond question the best harbor on the whole coast of Porto Rico. It is deep inland, with enough depth of water to carry any vessel in ordinary shipping. It is the bay where the American army first landed, when the invasion commenced, and by building pontoon docks out 225 feet, all stock was unloaded from the transports with ease. It is almost a model harbor, and with small expense can be put in perfect condition, as it practically already has depth enough and is completely protected from the sea.

It may become the principal trading port of the island, when roads and railroads are completed throughout.

The harbor of San Juan, the capital, is of ample size

A Glimpse of the Road Between Ponce and Port Ponce, Showing the Trains of Ox Carts Drawing American Army Supplies.

HARBORS.

and sufficient depth of water, but the channel leading to it is narrow and so difficult that the frequent storms of the north coast seriously interfere with San Juan's trade.

It is probable that the channel will be improved, as no doubt San Juan will remain the capital and principal town of the island. It has many great advantages, and with an improved harbor, will soon become an American city.

The other harbors, some of them hardly to be called harbors, Arecibo, on the north, Aguadilla and Mayaguez on the west, Guayanilla, Ponce and Arroyo on the south, and Humacao on the east, are nothing more than small pockets in the coast line, and some of them nothing more than open roadways in the ocean. Arecibo is exposed fully to the ocean and has no protection. A vessel cannot risk lying at anchor if a blow is on, but must put to sea. Ponce, Mayaguez, Aguadilla and Arroyo, are a little better, but will necessitate great outlay of money in building docks and moles or breakwaters strong enough to resist the enormous power of the ocean waves.

American capital will find a large field in the needed harbor improvements in all the ports of Porto Rico.

In Playa de Ponce, for instance, the warehouses seemed to be all wrongly located. They certainly are not near the place where the first shipping dock will be built. The Spanish administration seems to have taken absolutely no cognizance of the requirements and interests of commerce. At present there are no docks. Unloading is done by means of lighters, a mile or so out in the bay. Our American merchants will not stand the loss of time and the unnecessary expense of such a method very long.

MOUNTAINS, MINES, CAVES, ETC.

To those approaching Porto Rico from any direction, it appears to consist of nothing but mountains, and the aspect of the green terraced tiers, rising gradually from the coast to a height varying from 670 meters (2,233 feet) in the west to 1,520 meters (5,066 feet) in the north-east, is certainly beautiful and very attractive.

The highest peak is Mount El Yunque, 1,520 meters high and visible from the sea at a distance of sixty-eight miles. It is part of the range running east and west, and dividing the island into the north and south portions. The range extends from the capes of San

Battery M, 7th Artillery, Limbered Up Ready for Action, Two Miles West of Ponce, on the Road to Yauer.

Juan on the eastern extremity, to Point Cadera, near Rincon in the west. From this range, the great watershed of the island, the waters have run north and south for thousands of years, washing out deep ravines and valleys and leaving standing between them innumerable ridges, which in turn became small watersheds and were cut into by the torrents of the rainy season.

Notable high peaks are Torrecilla, between Barranquitas and Barros, 3,667 feet high; Mata de Platanos, near Penuelas, 3,030 feet high; Torito, in Cayey, 2,856 feet high; Silla de Guilarte, in Adjuntas, 2,660 feet high, and Cerro-Gordo, in San German, 2,233 feet high.

In minerals the little island cannot be expected to be very rich, but there are three salines (at Salinas, Guanica and Cabo Rojo), while galena is mined in La Rosita in Guayama; gold is washed in La Catinesterlila in Luquillo; lead is found in Guyama, and lime-phosphates on the island of Mona.

There are some thermal springs, the most famous among them being the Banos de Coamo, near Santa Isabel, in the south, where people afflicted with rheums and skin diseases find relief. The water here has a temperature of 113 degrees.

Two miles from Ponce are the sulphur baths of Quintana, the waters of which contain calcium and soda besides the sulphur. During the morning hours health-seekers enjoy the baths, while the afternoon and evening are given up to the sporting element.

The springs of Juana-Diaz have the reputation of strengthening an enfeebled stomach, and there are others in San Sebastian, San Lorenzo and Ponce, but their virtues do not seem to have been discovered or classified.

Of caves the island contains a large number. The interior of the most notable one, Aguas-Buenas, proves the volcanic origin of the island. It is tortuous, with deep recesses, but a visit is rendered unpleasant by clouds of bats inhabiting it, and whose droppings fill the cave to about one-third of its natural height. Of the other caves we will name two, that of Ciales, and in Arecibo the cave called Consejo, which is interesting to the geologist and traveller.

The Bath Houses at the Famous Quintana Springs, Near Ponce.

PUBLIC ROADS.

On account of the topography of the island, the public roads, which the government built principally from a military point of view, conform closely to the outline form of the island, making the circuit, with the exception of the south-east corner, while the south and north coasts are, in addition, connected by two roads running across the back of the big watershed. One of these, the road from San Juan to Coamo, is a splendid piece of engineering, and the pride of the inhabitants of the whole island. The road is about 100 kilometers or sixty-three miles long, and thirty feet wide, solidly built, macadamized and as smooth as anything except asphalt can be. From Coamo the road continues west through Ponce along the south shore, but although it is very good, it does not compare with the part first named.

The "royal roads," plainly indicated on our map, must be called very good as a whole, but outside of them there are absolutely no roads worth speaking of. What this must mean in such a mountainous region, where any road deserving the name can be built only at great expense, the reader will be able to imagine. From Mayaguez you may travel due east for thirty-five miles through a well-populated district before you reach a road, say at Utuado, and from there to Caguas, again due east, is about sixty miles between two good roads. There are roads connecting cities and villages, but they are so rough that a carriage or wagon would go to pieces in the first half hour, and in places you have to lead your pony over boulders and fallen trees for miles. Good roads will do wonders for the country, by opening up the interior.

In traveling through the island, you must be a good horseman to make one of these trips up the mountains. It is thrilling and grand if you can stay on your pony, as he climbs up and slides down the steep banks and wallows through the little rivers. I, myself, brought some marks of my trip back with me to the United States, in the shape of bruises.

When the rainy season sets in, the clay ground becomes so slippery, that the faithful animal, be it ever so honest, will lose its footing and sometimes give you a roll down the bank and land on top of you. This I tried to take as a joke because I was about the same size as my mount, and I simply acknowledged that it was a pony on me, and would lead him till we found

A Mountain Trip by Pony Path. (Fording a Stream.)

a better road. I shall never forget the impression I had, after climbing about two thousand feet above the sea, making eight miles on the back of a pony, when I turned and looked at the country behind me. We were in the midst of a coffee plantation and in view of the lower lands. We could see four small towns, and the capital in all her grandeur in the distance.

Certainly if you can endure the ride and are sure that you can stand a six hundred pound animal falling on you about three times, it will pay you to make such a trip. A more pleasing view, a more exhilarating atmosphere and a more restful place cannot be found. You are disturbed by nothing but the chatter of the few birds in the trees and these pass unnoticed, as the wild parrot does not talk our language; and the crow, if he ever had the caw of our American crow, has been compelled to leave it off and spends his time in studying the cut of your clothes.

If you desire to make an extended trip in Porto Rico, you may, of course, by taking plenty of time, cover a good part of the island by sailing around it and landing at different points, and then running inland as far as the roads are good, but this will take much more time, and will be much more expensive.

In this connection I should like to speak of an idea that occupied my mind frequently, as I travelled along the royal roads. All along these highways, at intervals of about six miles, there stand substantial buildings, erected for the purpose of sheltering the civil guards or military of the island.

These houses are constructed of masonry, about 20x40 feet. They are first-class buildings and by slight alterations could be made into most elegant public school houses. We shall not need them for the purpose for which they were erected, and as the people must have free schools, let our government, which went into this war with Spain for humanity's sake, import into the island some of our liberal-minded school teachers, of which we have enough and to spare, and open up all these good buildings as public schools, as soon as possible, since Spain has now vacated the land.

Spanish Barracks in San Juan, Showing the Effects of the Bombardment by the American Fleet on May 12, 1898.

RAILROAD AND STREET CARS.

The railroads of the island are all narrow gauge and not far reaching in length. The island is girdled by one franchise, which starts at the capital, San Juan, and were the road built, would carry you clear around the island, about 275 miles, touching all the towns along the coast, and at Humacao, on the east end of the island, a branch would run into Caguas about twenty-five miles, and there are nice dotted lines on the company's map to show where other branches may be run. As I said before, this is only a franchise. It was granted to a French company about eight years ago, and you must not go to Porto Rico expecting to ride around the island by rail for some two years to come. It will be taken care of by some of our enterprising Americans, and from some little facts I gathered I am confident that the first steps in this direction have already been taken. The franchise referred to has expired and is declared by good authorities to be perfectly worthless. The present tracks will be utilized so far as this can be done, but there will be a new grant, leaving the old company out.

When the franchise was granted eight years ago,

RAILROAD AND STREET CARS.

a start was made from the capital south to Bayamon, and thence west to Arecibo and a little beyond this point, which is in all about fifty miles. A start was also made at Aguadilla to Rincon, through Anasco and Mayaguez, and beyond, to within about two miles of San German, with a branch from Anasco to Lares. Another start was made at Ponce and carried through Guayanilla to Yauco, and also a short piece of road was built from San Juan toward Carolina, which lies east of the capital, but was not finished and has never been used. This is all that has been done in railroad building, and as it rests to-day, is absolutely useless to the public. Out of the whole franchise of about 300 miles, only about 134 miles have been constructed. The gauge of the road is 3 feet $11\frac{1}{4}$ inches. The road is well equipped with rolling stock and the depots and water tanks all along these pieces of road are of masonry and in good condition. The incompleteness of the system and the irregular running of trains exclude all freightage and keep the usefulness of the road down in every way. The roadbed looks as much like a pasture as like a railroad. In fact, stock may be seen along the tracks, and in fifty miles our engineer slackened his sixteen-mile-an-hour speed more than

Railway Depot and Yards at Ponce.

once to give some huge ox or bull the privilege of crossing, as the animal was weightier than the engine. Trains are run only in the early morning and late afternoon hours. From 10 a. m. to 4 p. m. there is no traffic.

This will all soon, and very soon, be changed. American business methods are bound to bring good results in this, as in all other directions. The enterprising early visitors on the island seemed to prefer a cold franchise to flowers, oranges and pretty things, as the franchises were well looked to before they had seen a plantation in the land. When we were in Ponce, about the time the protocol was signed, it was truly amusing to see the crowd of speculators gathering there, and all of them trying to get on the inside of something good. Not one of them seemed to realize the insignificant size of the island and had they compromised the matter by agreeing to divide up on the whole franchises and each take an equal share, they would not have gotten more than about eleven feet each.

From the capital to Rio Piedras runs a narrow gauge railroad to accommodate the small suburban travel, and to haul grass. By the way, Rio Piedras is the summer resort of the capital; the governor-general's summer home is there among others. This short road would make a nice electric line and will undoubtedly be used in this way in the near future.

In Mayaguez, the west end town, there is a little toy street car line from the harbor up to the street on which the town hall is situated. It is the only real street car line on the island. The cars are drawn by little ponies, and are so small that but few people can ride at a time. If a car jumps the track, the conductor and driver invite the people aboard to leave the car, and then they lift it back on the rails. I don't know who owns the road, but think it is a syndicate of residents of the town. Directly after our people took possession of Mayaguez on the 12th of August, the board of directors of this extensive enterprise notified the public that instead of the 3-cent fare that had been charged up to that time, they were compelled to charge now 5 cents, assigning as the reason that the great increase in business necessitated it, as the management had to exert themselves so much more to fill the demands on them. It was perhaps good argument, but it looked to my skeptical mind more as if

Engine and Train, Narrow Gauge Road Between San Juan and Arecibo.

the owners had heard of Wall street and were taking advantage of an opportunity.

Whether American capitalists will find profitable fields in Porto Rico in the way of street car lines, I cannot say; but until the interior is opened up more and until wages for labor—now 60 to 70 cents a day—shall have risen to a higher standard, I should say there will not be people enough who want to ride to make any new surface road pay anywhere on the island.

TELEGRAPH AND TELEPHONES.

From the capital you can communicate with all the principal towns of the island by telegraph, both around the coast and throughout the interior. It was estimated that at the time our army invaded the island, there were in use about 500 miles of telegraph line. It can be said of the telegraph in Porto Rico that it was found in more perfect working order than any other branch of public improvements, and it will need but few additions to make the system complete. As in European countries, the telegraph lines were built and controlled by the government, and were, therefore, like the royal roads, well planned and constructed at the expense of the people. This method has one advantage: As the people have paid the cost of establishing the plant, they are not called upon to pay more for the service than it takes to run the system. The rates are consequently so low as to be a surprise to an American.

The telephone is not in universal use in the island, but is making fair progress. We found it in quite general use in the three principal towns. In San Juan the residents estimated that there were 500 'phones in use; in Ponce 200, and more being added daily, and in Mayaguez it was coming into general use. The telephone is destined to play a prominent part in the affairs of the island in a short time. The towns are not far distant from each other, and a simple little line, such as is needed to do business from place to place will cost little. A system reaching from shore to shore north and south and even east and west will not cost much, and I doubt not that each and every town will soon have the telephone and through this means of communication the island will be much benefited.

A Street in Ponce.

MEASURES AND MONEY.

Like the Spanish mother country, the colony of Porto Rico used nominally and officially the metric system, but the common people, of course, are slow everywhere to adopt anything new in the line of the abstract. In our own country the marketmen in the east still talk of "a shilling a pound," meaning thereby $12\frac{1}{2}$ cents in New York, and 16 2-3 cents in Boston.

The royal roads and the railroads are measured, therefore, by kilometers (1,000 meters equal .62137 of a mile), and the milestones of Porto Rico are kilometer posts. In trading at the shops, however, the meter is not in use, but the old Spanish vara, shorter by three inches and a fraction than our yard. The vara has thirty-six pulgadas or inches. The square vara is used for measuring land. Seventy-five varas square are called a cuerda, which is a little less than our acre. The weights are the same as ours.

The monetary system is decimal, like ours. A peso has 100 centavos, but is worth only about 50 cents, American money. The coins in circulation are of the following denomination: 1 centavo and 2 centavos of copper; 5, 10, 20, 40 centavos and 1 peso of silver, and 5 and 10 pesos in gold. The latest coins all bear the imprint "Isla de Puerto Rico," but they were minted in Spain. Of paper currency they have 5, 10 and 20 pesos bills. The fives are of the size and shape of a cabinet photograph; the tens are considerably larger, and the twenties are of commercial letter size. The bills I saw were made in the United States.

Of course this money will be speedily replaced by our United States currency. We shall have to shoulder the expense of cancelling and withdrawing the coins and substituting ours for them. What will become of the bills I cannot say, but there will probably be no difficulty about it, and no loss entailed to anybody.

During the author's sojourn in the island a local paper (a curiosity, printed on one side of a sheet $12\frac{1}{2}$ inches by $8\frac{1}{2}$ inches, without date or indication of the place of publication, called El Buscapie—Footguide), contained a leader, in which it was stated that a New York moneyed company intended to buy up all the Porto Rican pesos at \$1 each, to make souvenirs of the war of them and sell them, making a profit of about \$2,000,000 on them and relieving the Porto Ricans of a serious and embarrassing problem.

Custom House, Port Ponce. Gens. Miles' and Wilson's Headquarters During the Invasion.

Our saying of "castles in Spain" has, of course, its equivalent in Spanish. Could it be that this equivalent is anything like "gold mines in New York"?

MISCELLANEOUS INFORMATION.

COAL has not yet been discovered on the island except in insignificant quantities, and it is not believed that there is much of it there. What is used comes from Norfolk, Va., and costs $8\frac{1}{2}$ to 10 pesos per ton. Only the electric light plants, factories, railroads, etc., requiring a constant supply of coal, have occasion to purchase it. All cooking is done by charcoal, brought down from the mountains by the peons and selling at 25 centavos per bushel.

BRICKS are rather poor in quality, being soft and easily broken, though durable when laid in the wall. They are made of a size about 6x9x1¼ inches. They are commonly sold in the towns at 8 pesos per 1,000 delivered. The supply of clay is unlimited.

PAINTS.—Way up in the mountains, 2,000 feet above the sea, about seven miles south of Rio Grande, are found in abundance the minerals used for paint, in red, white and blue. These colors are displayed on the buildings, throughout the island, with scarcely any variation, either by mixing them together or adding other shades. It is curious indeed that Mother Earth should, in this island, supply the colors which represent, so completely, our national emblem—the stars and stripes. The people of Porto Rico will value henceforth, more than ever, this chalky substance, because it will serve as a reminder of the flag that relieved them from the oppression endured by them for centuries.

LUMBER.—The duty on lumber up to this time has been 4 pesos on rough, and 6 pesos on dressed. The prices at which lumber has retailed run from 28 pesos for the commonest pine to 45 pesos for good Georgia pine. The island produces some beautiful hardwood, highly prized for furniture. Some of it sells in the log for 5 pesos per cubic foot in the harbors.

GALVANIZED CORRUGATED IRON is used generally throughout the island for roofs and temporary enclosures. Heretofore it has been principally imported from England, and is now selling for 6 pesos and 25 centavos per 100 pounds, being sold in bundles of fourteen sheets, 3x6 feet, with an average weight of 220 pounds a bundle. It stands the climate well, notwithstanding many reports to the contrary.

Camp of Battery C, Pennsylvania Boys, Near Quintana Springs.

MISCELLANEOUS INFORMATION. 125

LABOR.—Native workmen (peons) on the plantations are furnished, without expense, a thatched shanty, usually containing one room. They have also the use of a small plot of ground for a garden. They work by the year at from 8 to 20 pesos per month, and are always in debt to their employers, who oblige them to take their pay out in goods kept in a small store or commissary run by each planter.

Carpenters, bricklayers and the more skilled laborers have had but little work in the past year or two, but when employed get from $1\frac{1}{2}$ to 2 pesos per day.

RATES OF INTEREST.—Ordinary commercial paper, running six months or less, is usually drawn at from 10 to 12 per cent. Short loans from $1\frac{1}{2}$ to 2 per cent. per month; long time loans on real estate, three to five years, from 9 to 12 per cent. Long time loans are secured by mortgages which are in current use, as in the United States.

REGISTRY OF DEEDS.—Only about 10 per cent. of all property holdings are recorded. Not until about 1880 was a system of registry adopted and made a law, and the requirements of the law are so expensive, in the surveys and other charges, that only a few have availed themselves of its benefits. Titles generally are considered good when proper transfers have been made, which means getting the signatures of all the living people who might in any way become heirs to the seller. The recording does not seem to give any advantage, except as a safeguard against the loss of the papers.

RENTS.—The rate of rent charged for any property seems to be established at about 12 per cent. of its cost or earning power capitalized. If the house cost 1,200 pesos and the lot were valued at 800 pesos, the rent at 12 per cent. would be 240 pesos a year.

SOME STRIKING PECULIARITIES OF PORTO RICAN LIFE.

ICE, artificially made, is only to be obtained in three towns: San Juan, Ponce and Mayaguez. The price is from 20 to 30 pesos per ton in large quantities, and from 2 to 6 centavos per pound at retail. The natives use but little, and since the American occupation the army has utilized the plants to their utmost capacity, frequently no ice being obtainable at any price.

BUTTER is not made on the island. The small quantity used is brought from Denmark and Holland, and costs 1 peso per pound. It comes in sealed packages.

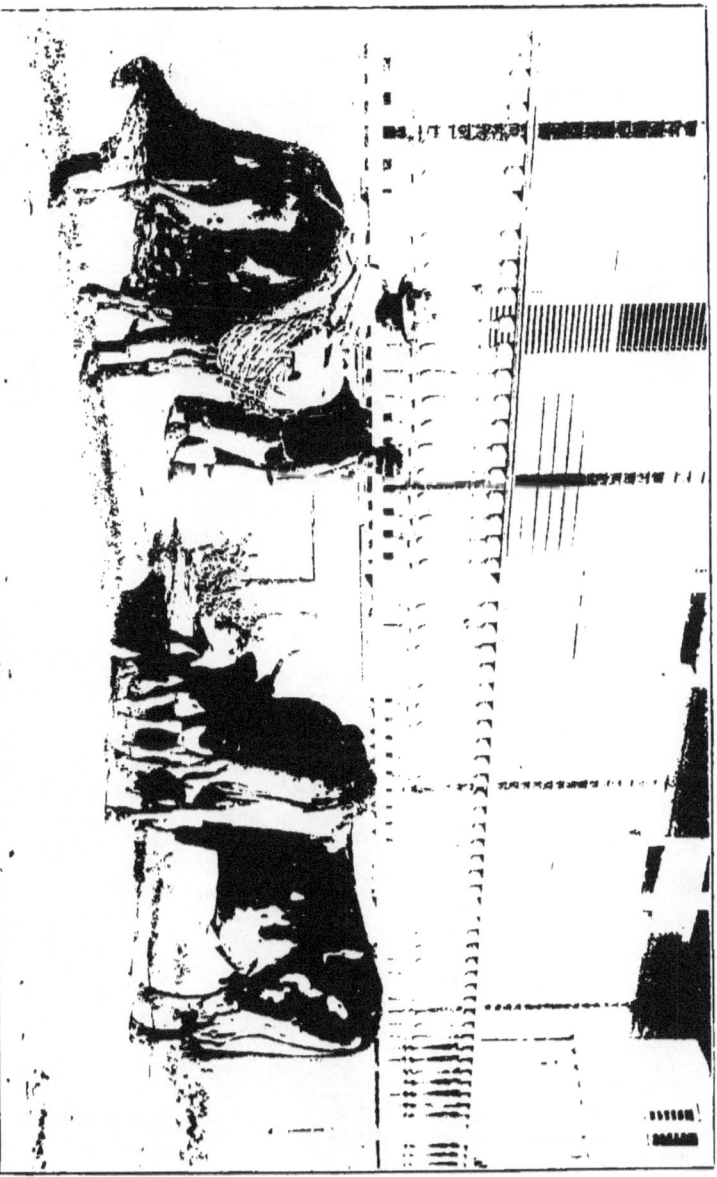

The Porto Rican Milkman, Driving the Cows From Door to Door.

The scarcity of butter makes the problem of eating a serious one for Americans, as one is obliged to become accustomed to many unfamiliar dishes. Olive oil and garlic reign supreme. A native cannot eat unless his food is flavored with odorous garlic and swimming in oil. When we forbade our cook to further use these articles, she said, straightening up, that it was impossible to prepare a meal without them.

PEDDLING MILK.—In many of the towns the milkman drives his cow from door to door calling out "vaca" (cow), and his customers generally bring out a large bottle and watch the fluid milked into it. The calf always accompanies the cow. The peddler cannot be accused of watering his milk unless they think him expert enough to carry a supply up his sleeve. I saw one of our soldiers buying milk, who, after seeing it drawn from the cow accused the milkman of selling him agua (water). I wondered whom the charge was against, the man or the cow. The cow looked unconcerned, I am sure, but the milkman did not, although I could not swear that he understood the Yankee's joke any better than his fourfooted milk can did.

WATERING THE STREETS.—The island being so rich

in mountain streams, it is no wonder that many of the cities have water-works. The streets are sprinkled by a man going from point to point, opening a small trap in the narrow walk, attaching a hose to a water main and squirting a thin stream as far as the force will reach.

A FUNERAL in Porto Rico is as simple and unpretentious as it can be made. The rank or circumstances of the family who suffers loss by the death of a member, may be judged in watching a procession to the cemetery. The poorer are carried to their last resting place by their friends and sometimes on the heads of a couple of sturdy peons. The next class, or middle class will enjoy the luxury of a cart, and the higher class will resort to the extravagance of a hearse. In no case do the women or children attend the funeral of a native or a Spaniard. Sometimes when a funeral of a foreigner is held, they will turn out, but this does not occur often.

THE CEMETERIES are a curiosity. They are partly walled in and the walls are thick enough to have tiers of recesses, in which the coffins are deposited. The poorer people rent one of these vaults for five years for 25 pesos, the well-to-do buy one or several outright,

A Porto Rican Funeral Procession.

The Tiers of Vaults in a Cemetery.

while only the very richest families aspire to a private tomb. In our picture of the cemetery of Ponce, the reader may notice, on the seal of the vault in the right-hand lower corner, the letters R. I. P., signifying: *requiescat in pace;* or "may he rest in peace." When I first noticed this inscription, I wondered in my mind whether I was the lucky discoverer of the grave of Rip Van Winkle, but the remainder of the name dispelled my ludicrous fancy at once, of course. The letters met my eyes many times more in that cemetery.

THE HOUSES are mostly built of brick, and stuccoed. One story is the rule. Glass panes for windows are unknown. Slats take their places.

THE STORES have no show-windows, but, as shown in our cuts, nothing but doors, three or four of which lead into the same room, to be used either as a store or shop or dwelling, according to the tenant's needs.

One of our cuts shows the polite Spanish way of protecting the walls of their houses from the disfiguring poster. Instead of our forbidding "Post no bills!" you find the notice that "You may post your bills at the rate of 25 pesos each."

AN OBJECT LESSON.

In presenting the two pictures, one of the Spanish, the other of American officers, taken while the armies were in service in Porto Rico, we call attention to the striking contrast in bearing and difference in dignity of the two forces. This difference is so impressive as to be an object lesson to the world of to-day, and to all coming generations.

The Spanish officers are pitiable specimens of soldiers, with their frail bodies and half child-like bearing, in their humiliation and dependency, with all manhood blasted by superstition and tyrannical government. The American officers, on the other hand, have won the admiration of the world. Instead of looking the humble insubordinate, every man is a knight, brave and true. Their tall, muscular frames, their bright faces and their dare-devil courage, is the product of the free schools of America.

Surely these two pictures may stand as forcible illustrations of the truth, to be learned by every man, woman, boy and girl, that governments, like individuals, are known by their fruits. One teaches the folly of bad government, while the other is a

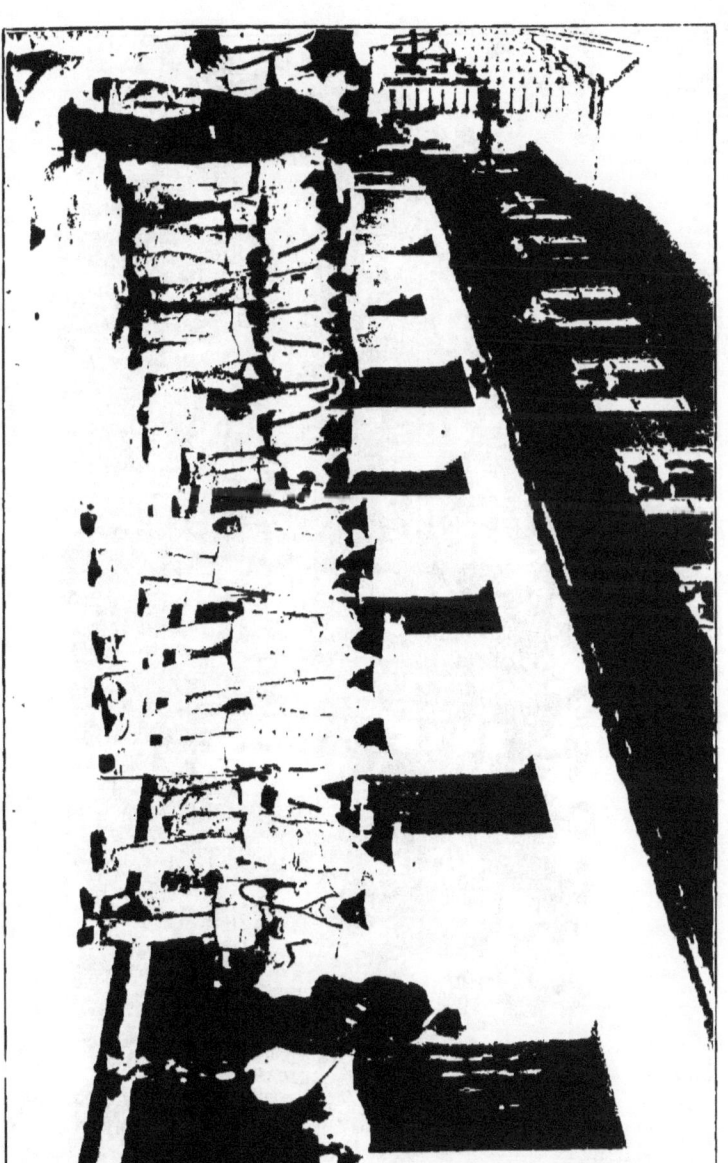
Group of Spanish Officers and Soldiers in Arecibo. The Officer on Horseback was Commander of the Port.

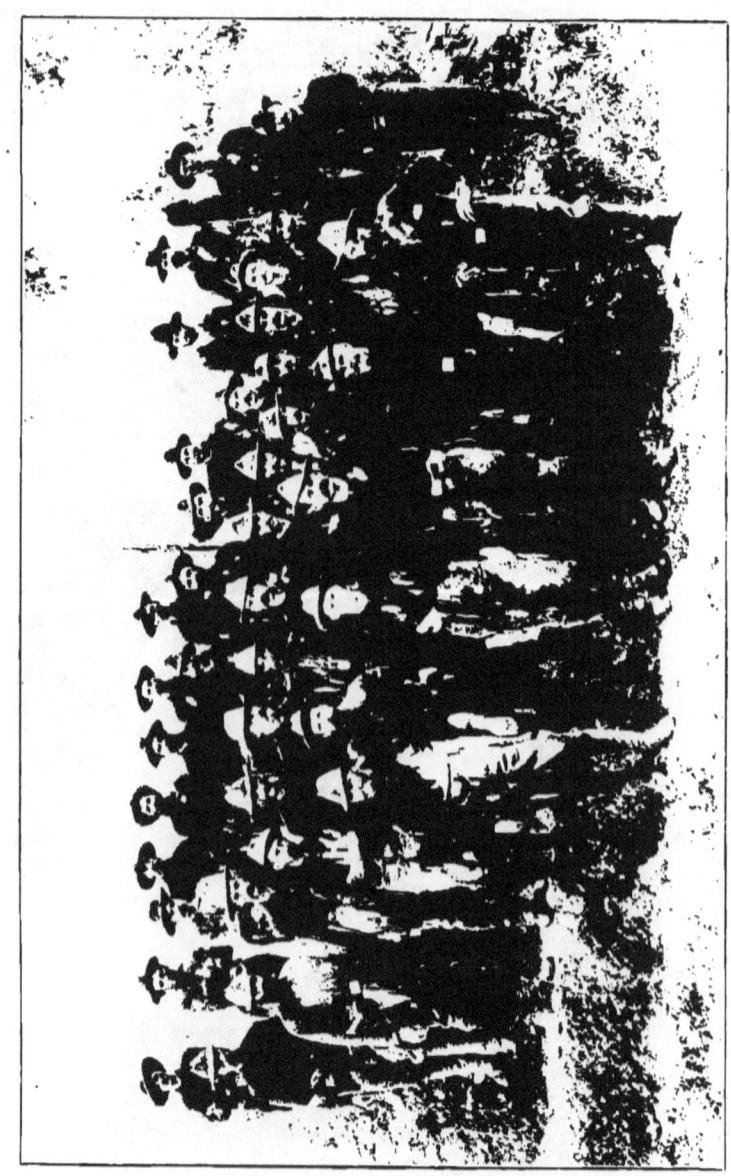

Officers of the 6th Ills., Who Did Such Excellent Service in Porto Rico. Tall Figure in Front Line is Col. Jack Foster.

splendid apotheosis of the blessings of our free institutions and self-government.

THE MARKET OF PONCE.

The daily supply of food is always procured at the market, where from 6 o'clock to 10 A. M. each day, Sunday included, the servants of all the wealthy families and the mistresses and children of the poor, repair for the purchase of their daily supplies. The grocery stores are chiefly concerned in the sale of liquors, of various canned goods, condiments, and such articles as are not perishable. There are no meat markets, no refrigerators and no ice except in cafes of the better class, and even there only in homoeopathic quantities.

The market in Ponce is an iron-roofed building, open on all four sides to the elements, surrounded by enormous stone pillars, with a floor of cement, and the entire square surrounding it is paved with blocks of native dressed stone. In the interior of the market are hundreds of little stalls, or booths, leased by the municipality and presided over by a market-master and native policemen, who enforce order.

On one side is the fish market, in which a great

variety of fish are exposed for sale. At one place a steak will be carved for you from an enormous sturgeon; in another, large red snappers are exposed for sale, whole or by the pound; in others, small fish, freshly caught, are for sale by the string, usually six to eight strung together, and offered for from 20 to 25 centavos. All the fish in these waters are beautifully marked; one variety is a deep red, almost crimson; another will be gold, about twice as large as the gold fish of the aquaria, and several varieties of silver fish. There are no fish in any way similar to those of the United States, and perhaps the most marked characteristic of them all is their unusual coloring.

On the other side of the market meat is sold, all native—beef, pork, mutton and poultry. The native marketmen have not learned to cut up beef across the grain, but slice off a slab indiscriminately, with or across the grain, as the case may be, and it is all sold at a uniform price, the customers seemingly having no preference as to the cut, the choicest of steaks going at the same price as the coarser portions.

In another section of the hall are fruits; in another vegetables, in another laces, tinware, hardware, hosiery, gay ribbons, shoes, in fact a department store,

Busy Scene in the Market Place of Ponce.

THE MARKET OF PONCE. 141

though owned by a hundred eager, screaming individuals, each one crying his or her wares as loudly as possible.

I asked the prices of many things, as they were sold in small portions that morning, with the following result. Musk melons, the kind our grandmothers raised, long, deeply-ribbed and yellow, 25 cents each; half-grown chickens, 75 cents per pair; eggs, 3 and 4 cents each; home-made cheese, similar to the good Dutch or cottage cheese, 10 cents a pound; guava jelly, 25 cents per pound; pine-apples, 10 to 20 cents each, according to size; bunches of bananas, 50 cents to $1; coarse brown sugar, 6 to 8 cents per pound; a lighter colored sugar, 8 cents per pound; refined white sugar is unknown; shelled corn, 4 cents per pound; American ham and bacon, each, 20 cents per pound; flour from New York, 8 cents per pound; home-made hard soap, 20 cents per pound; small head of cabbage, 20 cents each; guavas, 40 cents a peck; jerked beef from South America, 16 to 20 cents per pound; bread, 12 cents per loaf, weighing about a pound and a half; fresh rolls, 10 cents per dozen; small tomatoes, 1 cent each; oranges, 50 cents per hundred; white beans, 6 cents per pound; corn meal, 6 cents per pound; southern cow pears, 2 cents per pound; Irish potatoes, 8 cents per pound; sweet potatoes or yams, 2 cents per pound; native coffees, 20 cents to 25 cents per pound; cocoanuts, 3 cents each; fresh beef, 14 cents; pork and mutton, 20 cents. The above prices of course were all in Porto Rican money, which would make the articles about half the price named in American money.

In addition to these articles, I noticed the following, but was unable to procure the prices: Egg plant, gumbo, lima beans, small water melons, canapas, plantains, limes, pumpkins, summer and winter squashes, pomegranates, native peppers of a dozen sorts, live pigs, big and little, with their legs tied, lying in passive rows on the pavement awaiting purchasers, large field corn, sugar cane, string beans, garlic, more garlic, and plug tobacco in ropes at 25 cents per yard; cigarettes, 1 and 2 cents per bundle of ten; cigars from 1 to 5 cents each, the cheaper being equal to the dearer in quality, there as elsewhere.

From 6 o'clock to 10 pandemonium reigns; after that the crowd of purchasers dwindles away one by one, and the place is silent, and the attendants put up the shutters, sweep the floors and a torrent of water

Market Hall, Ponce.

Bird's-eye View in San Juan, the Capital of Porto Rico, Showing Governor's Mansion and Sea Wall on the Point, and two American Warships at Extreme Left.

is turned on through hydrants and everything is scrubbed to absolute cleanliness and the place is deserted till the next morning.

THE CAPITAL.

The capital, San Juan, according to the last census, had a population of 32,800. It is really a beautiful town, built on a peninsula, or, rather, an island, that runs almost directly west and out into the ocean. It is walled on the north or ocean side with strong fortifications, Morro Castle and San Cristobal fortresses, which will stand for ages to come, and which simply smiled at Sampson's famous bombardment. These gigantic walls, while there was some damage done in the city, might truthfully say, like the boy, "Never touched me."

Notable buildings are the "Beneficencia," the Lunatic Asylum, the Captain-General's Palace, the Administration Building (Intendencia), the Spanish Bank. the Barracks de Ballaja, the House of Representatives, the Civil and the Military Hospital, the Consistory, the Cathedral, other churches and the bishop's palace, the Institute for Secondary Education, and a seminary for the aspirants to priesthood.

The town is well paved throughout with white paving brick and is in the best condition. It is exceptionally clean in outward appearance, as the streets are on such an incline that the frequent showers of rain dash all the dirt off and down into the bay. Good telegraph and telephone service, gas works, electric light works, ice factory and some other small manufacturing plants give the town a decidedly modern aspect. It is destined to remain the principal town of the island. By reclaiming some low land, dredging some natural lagoons, improving some little islands and extending the drives, the district south of the present town could be made one of the handsomest tropical parks in the world.

Before I visited the place I said, "If we took Porto Rico, we should destroy the wall around the north of San Juan." I have changed my mind—we should not destroy it, but should keep it for its picturesqueness and for the story it tells of the past 400 years. As a protection, it is of less value now than ever, as we Americans prefer to rely on our boys and their marksmanship.

Ample room may be found in the barracks for all the soldiers we shall need there and I think we shall

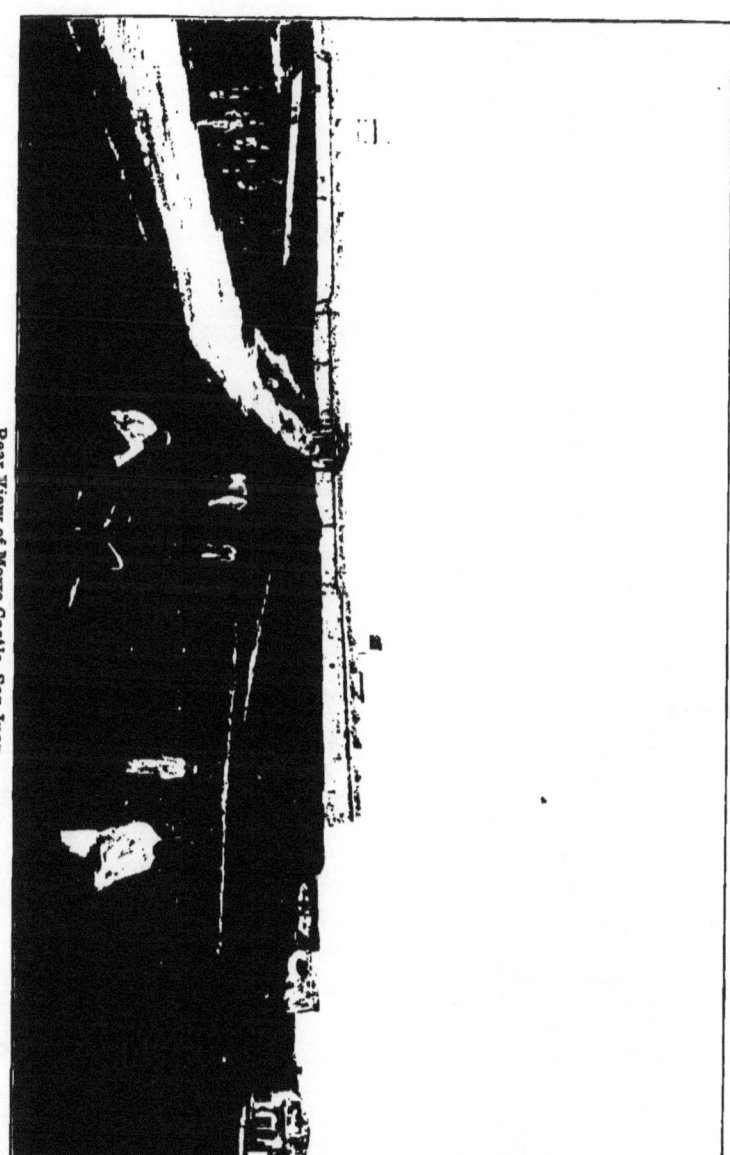

Rear View of Morro Castle, San Juan.

have space to let. They are at present constructing water works to bring water into the town, carried in iron pipes from a mountain stream. When this improvement is completed and if sanitary principles are observed, there will be no reason why San Juan should not be a very healthful and attractive place, especially as there will be no longer need of cramming the people together for the sake of retaining so large a part of the island for military purposes.

A LEGEND.

The pious people in Porto Rico are blessed with the presence of a miracle-working image, the history of which they love to tell, and in whose beneficial efficacy they place implicit confidence.

In the times when slavery was lawful and piracy lucrative, there lived a man in Porto Rico whose enterprise and shrewdness had made him immensely rich. When his fortune was large enough to satisfy him he turned his mind to other things. He wished now to acquire a standing among his countrymen and with heaven, and to this end he had to cleanse himself of the stains which his unrighteous life had left upon his reputation. This was accomplished by donating to the cathedral in Mayaguez the statue of a saint, carved and decorated in the most sumptuous style that the island afforded.

This image one day mysteriously disappeared from its resting place in the church. At first, people thought that thieves had sacrilegiously laid hands on the holy image, tempted by the rich jewels with which it was hung, and the whole population set out to discover the hiding place of the thieves and their booty. After many days of fruitless search, the image was accidentally discovered in the fork of a large tree in the forest many miles from Mayaguez, and, strange to relate, not a single gem or jewel was missing, nor was the slightest injury done to the statue itself or its decorations.

The happy people went out in solemn procession and carried their now doubly prized treasure back to their church in triumph. Speculation as to the perpetrators of the dastardly crime continued, but no clew to their identity was found. Hardly, however, had the excitement subsided, when one morning, on opening the church, the place of the statue was found to be empty again. Amazed and bewildered, the people never thought of going to the place where the

The Old Cathedral, Port Ponce, Where Battery C, Pa. Vols., Camped on Landing in Porto Rico.

saint had been recovered the first time, but there it was found after all, again by an accident, and again intact.

To make an end to such disturbances of the peace, the people now surrounded the church with soldiers and guards, placing a watch at every door and window, below and in the belfries, and threatening death to any of them who should be discovered asleep or careless at his post.

In spite of all these precautions, however, the saint went on the third escapade after a while, and was found again perched in the fork of the tree in the depth of the forest. Then it dawned upon the people that it could not be human hands that had removed the image, nor could they find any human purpose in these removals, and the grey-haired priest gave it as his opinion that the saint seemed to wish a change of location and that her desire should be granted, in return for which she would assuredly be gracious to the island and grant many a favor to those praying to her. This opinion was universally accepted by the good people of Porto Rico and a church was accordingly built in the place of the tree and the image was given the place of honor therein. The city of Hermogueras, according to the legend, sprung up around this new church.

The pious in Porto Rico firmly believe to this day in the healing power and benevolence of this image, as the pilgrimage of thousands annually testifies.

AN AMERICAN HERO'S GRAVE.

At Ponce, in the old cemetery, may be seen the grave of Ethan Allen, of the Second Wisconsin Volunteers. This grave is located about one-third the way through the grounds, on the right side of the main walk.

Allen undoubtedly was the first American soldier to be buried on the island. When our army, aboard the transports, steamed into Ponce harbor July 27th, 1898, he reported himself sick, and received the best care that could be given him. But in spite of all that could be done, he sank rapidly and in only a few hours was no more. He had answered his last bugle call; had performed his last good service; had done all he could do—given his life for his country.

On the same day that Allen died, the town of Ponce was surrendered to the Americans, and arrangements were made to bury the comrade of the brave Wiscon-

General View of Cemetery in Porto Rico.

sin boys in the cemetery. An undertaker was secured, together with two carriages, and on the 28th of July, all that was earthly of brave Ethan Allen was carried to the burying ground and after firing the customary salute, was placed in a grave. The remains of this brave boy lie there to-day under the tropical flowers, 2,500 miles from home, where his officers and comrades were compelled to leave them.

This pathetic little story is related because poor Allen was the first to fall and in telling this incident it is applicable to many of our worthy, uncomplaining boys in blue who went to Porto Rico at the call of their country, but never returned to their loved ones at home.

For the family and friends of our soldiers who lost their lives in the service, there is the great consolation that they wore their uniform with credit; they died as only the brave can die, and that every one of them was an honor to the mother, sister or sweetheart who blessed them and was so proud when they marched away.

THE RED CROSS.

Not as part of the history of Porto Rico do we speak of the Red Cross Society, but its work has been of so much importance in the invasion by the Americans, that we feel it should have a place in our attempt to picture the island as we found it. The work of the members of this society can never be fully described. The sacrifices they make and hardships they endure to carry relief to the suffering soldier boys in the field is deserving of the heartfelt gratitude of every true American.

Their work is to provide the soldier in the service with many things which it is impossible for the army commissaries to furnish, and to comfort and nurse the sick and wounded. They did their work well in this war, as thousands of our brave boys will testify, who enjoyed the delicacies of light, nourishing diet, which took the place of hard tack and side meat. They knew no nationality or sect in their work, but stood on the humane platform of love for all mankind, as ready to relieve the suffering of the unfortunate Spaniard as of one of our own fallen heroes. At the latter part of the war the Spanish Red Cross officials and

Scene in Spanish Hospital in San Juan. Spanish and American Red Cross Doctors and Nurses Together with Sick and Wounded Spanish Soldiers. Rev. H. F. Barnes, of Boston, Agent for the Red Cross, is Shown Wearing the White Mark on the Left Arm.

Ambulances of American Army in Camp After the Protocol was Signed.

ours met and consulted together. Thousands are the stories that could be told by our boys, of how their burning heads were cooled by some sacrificing nurse who left her home and travelled 2,000 miles, and more, to render this noble service, and whose touch was like the mother's or sister's.

The Red Cross will never be forgotten by those who witnessed their good work—God bless them.

A SPANISH OFFICER'S SWORD.

Just after the Americans entered Mayaguez and while the neighboring towns were still held by the Spanish, no one, of course, was permitted to go beyond our pickets without a pass from the Spanish governor-general. But this did not stop a certain American who was determined to see the next town. He was challenged by the Spanish sentries, the guard was called out, and the commanding officer ordered him to return at once from where he had come. The American politely informed the officer that he knew he was talking to a gentleman, and rather than do anything that might make trouble for any one, he would leave the town if he had to walk. The Spaniard replied that his desire to oblige a gentleman was in conflict with his duty. After some further exchanges of civilities they concluded they were both good fellows and adjourned to a place where refreshments were served, to settle further details. They took brandy, "limonada" and cigars, and then "limonada," cigars and brandy, followed up by the best dinner the house could afford, at the American's expense, with free music, furnished by the landlord's pretty daughter.

The point at issue was not wholly forgotten in this flood of good things; the discussion of the question, whether the American was under arrest or not, alternating with a contemplation of the war from a reasonable standpoint. While the Spaniard imbibed his brandy and did justice to the dinner, his patriotism rose to an admirable pitch and he remarked: "I am under orders to surrender this town in about two weeks with all army effects, but, sir, I shall never surrender this sword. I shall break it and throw the pieces into the sea. I have sworn to wear it with honor to my country, and to die rather than yield it into other hands." "Oh! I would not break it," said the American; "I will tell you what to do. You have worn it with honor to your country and yourself; now

Spanish Transports Lying in the Harbor of San Juan, Ready to Take the Spanish Army Home.

let me honor both the sword and you. Let me take it back to America. I will hang it on the wall of my library and many will be the good drinks I shall take and the cigars I shall smoke to the soldier and gentleman who honored that sword by wearing it. I will tell the story to the young generation, and it will give to the world a lesson in patriotism and generosity."

The officer seemed impressed by the argument and the same evening the American was escorted to his train and allowd to depart, instead of sleeping in a prison cell. Just before the train pulled out, a carriage drove rapidly up and the officer, who is the principal in this little story, stepped out and handed the American a package, bidding him "a Dios." Upon examination, the American found the package contained the valued sword. It now hangs in the library of a prominent young Chicago lawyer, who would not sell it for many times its real value.

A TYPICAL HACIENDA OWNER.

About nine miles due east of Mayaguez, on the road to Lares, there lives Lope Valdestino Pelissier, owner of a 200-acre coffee plantation. He is a rich man for Porto Rico, but lives, with his family, in a very plain fashion, though with the pride of a knight and the manners of a perfect gentleman. At the gateway of his mountain home, seven Americans halted their ponies in August, 1898, partly to seek shelter from one of those drenching mountain showers, and partly to rest and draw on the hospitality of the owner for refreshments.

The interpreter of the party addressed the dignified old gentleman, asking if he could favor them with dinner, and he replied with great politeness that his poor, mean home was at their disposal, that they were welcome to all he could do for them.

The dinner was prepared (and a splendid dinner it was), and in pleasant conversation an hour was passed at the table. After the meal was ended, one of the guests proffered an American $10 bill in payment, but the planter told them that he believed he was entertaining gentlemen and friends, and that he could not

A Rich Man's Plantation, and Lane Leading to the Mansion.

A Peon's Home Under the Shelter of Banana Trees.

think of accepting money; and even if they were not friends, he could make no charge, as he was not an innkeeper.

The family of this generous Spaniard was most interesting. The eldest daughter, about 20 years of age, was strikingly beautiful with her dark hair and great blue eyes. One of the party presented her with a small silk American flag, which she at once placed in her hair. This flag seemed to add to her attractiveness, as the red was like her rosy lips and cheeks, and the blue like her limpid eyes. Never was the flag worn more proudly by an American than by this Porto Rican girl. I venture to say, no more valuable citizen will be found anywhere than the owner of this hacienda, if one may judge from such short acquaintance.

SPANISH SINCERITY.

In Ponce, in the early days of the American invasion, when things were very much unsettled, some of the fastidious diners, who were not used to having garlic and olive oil in all the dishes placed before them and who felt they could not live if entirely cut off from everything like a club or the fine eating houses in the United States, clubbed together for renting a house, that they might be able to have their own meals prepared and to give their orders in English. The standing order, or, rather, supplication was, "For God's sake, leave out the garlic and olive oil."

One party of three, in a case of this kind, started out one morning, determined to secure quarters and make arrangements for preparing their next meal. After many inquiries and much walking they were finally directed to the house of a Spanish professor. A more pleasant gentleman could not be found. He tendered the use of five rooms without charge and made daily calls, offering his services in any way he might be useful.

As the days passed, a warm friendship grew up between the Spaniard and Americans, many amusing incidents resulted from the mixed conversations, in the efforts to understand each other—the professor at all times exerting himself to master the English. The war was discussed and the causes which led to the bitter conflict, the Spanish gentleman being outspoken in his views, giving in full the opinions he held previous to the war. He said: "I was born and raised in Spain and my mother still lives there, and it is but natural that I should be attached to the land of my

Camp of Battery M, United States Regular Army, on Road Between Yauco and Ponce.

birth. I felt that the Americans were unwarranted in invading our land; you would have felt the same way were you in my place. We Spaniards did feel bitter and no just man will censure us when he understands our position and learns how the Americans were represented to us. It is all over now; we find the Americans to be gentlemen, such as we claim to be, and such gentlemen as we can welcome into our homes. We now accept the situation as it is, hoping it will be for the better, and trying to believe it will be. My good old mother will perhaps die in Spain, while I shall remain in Porto Rico. I shall master the English language, become an American citizen, abide by the new laws, and the one great wish of my life shall be, that my 3-year-old boy shall grow up to be a worthy, respected citizen of the victorious, liberal and progressive United States, and that he may always love the stars and stripes, as my mother and myself have loved the flag of Spain."

A similar case occurred among another group of Americans, who, having taken a house, had just become comfortably settled, when one evening a gentleman entered who was readily recognized as a Spaniard. He addressed the party in fair English, stating that he lived next door, that he was a Spaniard, had been a Spanish sympathizer and would like to have seen Spain victorious, but that his holding these opinions did not necessarily bar them from being friends and that as they were strangers in the land and unacquainted with the customs, which would lead to many inconveniences, he had come to offer his services, hoping to be called upon if he could in any way add to their comfort. He proved of great service and a delightful neighbor.

AN EDITOR'S VIEW.

Just after the signing of the Protocol, an editorial appeared in the Porto Rican papers, in substance as follows: "We are confronted with a condition that is trying and sad, not to say humiliating. We have to meet the questions that loom up before us, and we must nerve ourselves to meet them as brave men and true, trusting women.

"It is sad, indeed, to think the time is coming, as come it must, for the Spanish to completely evacuate Porto Rico. It will be a trial and loss not only to those that go, but also to those that will stay. Many

American Boys Amusing Themselves After the Victory Had Been Won.

are the instances where old and dear friendships of long years' standing must be severed; where officers are to be sent away, who have resided here twenty years or more, who have married into our best families, and who have formed ties of love and friendship which were never meant to be severed. All of these families ties, and ties of dear friendship must now be broken, and our friends and dear ones must leave the land and deliver it over to the new power, which is practically unknown to us.

"It is not for us to pass judgment on the events that led up to the present situation, nor would it be profitable to do so. But it is proper that we pause to realize what we lose, and to look into the future. We give up what has been pleasant in the past, but we know not what the future may bring.

"It is our duty to ourselves, to meet our new fellow citizens, the Americans, frankly and without distrust. Let us welcome them as friends, let us welcome their laws and institutions, which they claim are so much more liberal and humane than ours, and let us trust that all will work out for the advancement of our interests and civilization. Let us welcome our conquerors and hope that our friendships with them may be lasting and true, and that sometime in the future we may again meet those that now leave us.

"We trust in the great wisdom of God, that all that now looks dark will not prove dark, and that we may all be gainers in the end."

LOOKING BACKWARD.

The patriotic Porto Rican of to-day does not deplore the events that brought about the change in political affiliation, by which he has become or is to become an American citizen. The burdens which impoverished Spain and were piled on the backs of her subjects and colonists were too heavy, not to give them a feeling of relief, now they have been taken away.

In order to realize the full weight of the burden, we must remember that Spain has always considered her colonies as milching cows from which to draw the greatest possible advantage, and at the smallest possible outlay. The Spanish system of exploiting her colonies consisted in sending to them armies of soldiery, priests, monks and civil officers, for whom the natives and later on the colonists had to provide shelter and food, and handsome salaries.

It became a settled institution in Spain to educate

the sons of noble families with a view to fill a government position in a colony, richly endowed and giving an opportunity, besides, for amassing a fortune rapidly, by taking bribes or stealing outright the funds contributed by the colonies or mother country for public improvements. To create such opportunities, great projects were always being carried out, roads constructed, cathedrals built in every little town, (seventy in Porto Rico), and contracts let for army supplies. To keep the colonists from rebelling against the enormous taxation, necessitated by the lavish equipment of the colonial administration, an army was kept, so large, that its disproportion to the needs of the colony in the way of protection against a foreign attack is almost ridiculous. Porto Rico is filled with splendid barracks and guard houses.

To this must be added the unnecessary sumptuousness of the civil and clerical establishments. The small island of Porto Rico had as extensive and elaborate a machinery of administration, as any monarchy in Europe. It was divided into seven provinces, besides which San Juan, the capital, formed a district by itself, similar to our District of Columbia. Each of the seven provinces had a governor, who was subordinate to the

Governor-General at the Capital. Each Governor had his staff of subordinates, and clerks, all imported from Spain.

The judiciary of the island have a separate and distinct plan of division. Eleven judicial circuits were laid out on the little island, each with a Superior Court over the local courts of the Alcalde and all of them subordinate to the Supreme Court and Court of Last Appeal for local affairs of San Juan.

The ecclesiastic diocese of Porto Rico consisted of twelve vicariates. The country fairly swarms with priests, many of them, no doubt, excellent men, and true friends of the lowly and poor, but the system of compelling the people to support this entire class in luxurious idleness, without a voice as to their number or character, is utterly wrong and must lead in too many cases to overbearing on the part of the supported, and to hatred on the part of the supporters.

Taxes and forced contributions swallowed up what little an ambitious workman might have laid up against a rainy day. It was useless to try to better one's conditions. There are no savings banks to speak of in Porto Rico. Is it a wonder that the population is indifferent and indolent? What incentive had the workman to save money, when he knew, that his little treasure would only rouse the covetousness of some priest or civil officer? What incentive had the planter to improve the road leading to his mountain recess, when he knew that his very secludedness was his only safety from the tax-gatherer and dishonest official?

LOOKING FORWARD.

The stars and stripes waving from San Juan will not increase the fertility of the Porto Rican soil; neither will the flag over Havana make Cuba raise more tobacco. Nothing but American thrift and industry will develop the agricultural and mineral resources of these islands.

The little red school house must bring to the Porto Ricans that mental training, which will enable them to enjoy the blessings of liberty as we understand and cherish it. This will take time. The present generation will but imperfectly appreciate and accept American ideas, and it will behoove us to use patience with them, but the boys and girls, now soon to come under the influence of our bright and devoted school teachers, will readily, and eagerly, seize upon the wider opportunities that we can afford them.

The author has endeavored to depict the island and the inhabitants as he found them, and shall feel gratified if he has succeeded in inspiring his readers with a love for the people from whose shoulders we have lifted the yoke, and with the firm belief that the new union will prove a blessing to them, and to us, and to all humanity.

A TIMELY, IMPORTANT BOOK

Laird & Lee's
PRACTICAL
Spanish Instructor

By F. M. De Rivas
A Graduate of the University of Seville, Spain

One sound for every letter. A unique method of learning Spanish without the aid of a teacher. Not a dictionary, phrase book or grammar. No irksome or confusing rules to be learned. Five thousand useful expressions; 2,000 names of Spanish officials, ships, cities etc., with their correct pronunciation.
Silk cloth, ... 25c
Morocco, full gilt, ... 50c

"It is especially to be commended for its lucid and comprehensive exposition of the pronunciation. . . . It has a complete list of syllables from which the Spanish words are formed, and also of officials, of diseases, of dishes ordinarily required, of verbs in common use, of occupations, arts, sciences, and all the acts and doings of everyday life."—*Carter's Monthly.*

The Book Correctly Spells and Pronounces all the Names of Places and Persons Used in "The Story of Beautiful Porto Rico."

You Make no Mistake in Purchasing a Copy.
The Best is Always the Cheapest.
For sale everywhere, or sent postpaid on receipt of price, by

LAIRD & LEE, 263 Wabash Av., Chicago

A BOOK OF
...INTERNATIONAL IMPORTANCE...

THE
Salva=Webster
Spanish=English & English=Spanish
384 Pages Dictionary Illustrated
40,000 Words and Definitions
New and Thoroughly Revised Edition

The Pronunciation of English Thoroughly Explained for Spanish Speaking Students of English.

Interlinear matter for practice of pronunciation in both languages; numerals, names of months, etc., grouped together; conversation pieces added, business and social correspondence enlarged. Also conversations, foreign moneys, colored maps, list of consulates, Spanish abbreviations, irregular verbs, Biographical and Geographical Cyclopedia, etc., etc., etc.

Invaluable to Business & Professional Men, Teachers & Students.

Capt. P. F. Harrington, of the Puritan, says: "Having some acquaintance with the Spanish language, I find the book an admirable one."

ENDORSED BY ARMY AND NAVY
PUBLIC AND PRESS

Should be in every library, public and private

Limp Cloth, No Index, 30c
Stiff Cloth, Double Index, Marbled Edges, 60c
For sale everywhere, or sent on receipt of price, by

LAIRD & LEE, 263 Wabash Av., Chicago

www.ingramcontent.com/pod-product-compliance
Lightning Source LLC
Chambersburg PA
CBHW032150160426
43197CB00008B/842